THE HANS POPPER COLLECTION
OF ORIENTAL ART

CENTER OF ASIAN ART AND CULTURE
San Francisco, California

> October 4 to November 18, 1973

WORCESTER ART MUSEUM
Worcester, Massachusetts

> December 10, 1973 to January 20, 1974

THE BALTIMORE MUSEUM OF ART
Baltimore, Maryland

> April 16 to May 26, 1974

CLEVELAND MUSEUM OF ART
Cleveland, Ohio

> July 10 to September 3, 1974

SEATTLE ART MUSEUM
Seattle, Washington

> September 20 to November 3, 1974

THE HANS POPPER COLLECTION
OF ORIENTAL ART

A Selection of 131 Chinese Ancient Bronzes,
Sculptures, Ceramics and Korean Celadons

By René-Yvon Lefebvre d'Argencé

Photography by Joe Schopplein

Produced by Kodansha International Ltd.

Copyright in Japan 1973, by Gretl Popper and Yvon d'Argencé
Printed in Japan
Library of Congress Catalogue Card Number 73–84623

Contents

Acknowledgements

THE completion of this catalogue was greatly facilitated by the extensive notes that Hans Popper made on every single piece in his possession. He was a researcher as well as a collector. Combined with Mrs. Popper's generous and enlightening guidance, his clear, systematic records were of considerable help. Mrs. Popper also took an active part in checking the photography and the layout of this catalogue. Her enthusiastic collaboration has been extremely valuable. I would also like to express my gratitude to Mr. J. E. Eskenazi of London who made available to me his files concerning a number of items in the Popper collection.

Particular thanks and credit must be given three members of the staff of the Center of Asian Art and Culture in San Francisco. Curator Diana Turner designed the chronological chart, compiled the bibliography, and was responsible for all the editorial work. Curator Yoshiko Kakudo wrote in the Chinese characters and checked on all Chinese and Japanese sources in the bibliography. My secretary, Carol Hansen, prepared the manuscript for printing.

All photographs, black and white as well as color, were taken by Joe Schopplein.

René-Yvon Lefebvre d'Argencé
Director and Chief Curator
Center of Asian Art and Culture
Golden Gate Park, San Francisco

Foreword

A thing of beauty is a joy forever:
Its loveliness increases; it will never
Pass into nothingness.

John Keats
(*Endymion*, Book I, Line 1)

MY husband came from a family in which interest and activity in the arts was something taken for granted. From early adolescence on, Hans attended concerts and took every opportunity to go to the theatre and to art exhibits. He learned to play the violin and became an excellent musician. His knowledge of musical history and literature was extraordinary. Music was always the art with which he intimately identified. Even in the midst of his business career, he found time to listen to concerts and to perform.

When we came to the United States in 1939 he had to devote much of his time to work, for this was a new beginning. We settled soon in San Francisco but his business took him to the Far East, a part of the world he had never seen before. He became fascinated with the arts of that area. Not that paintings, graphics and ceramics were new or strange to him—Hans' interest in them dated back to his days in Vienna where he enjoyed the modern art of the Expressionists—Klimt, Schiele, Kokoschka and others—along with the art of the "Old Masters". But Japanese and Chinese prints, scrolls and ceramics appealed to him in a special way and evoked in him a response and interest that gradually dominated his life. By that time—the late 1950's—he already had a considerable collection of paintings and drawings that included a number of works by French Impressionist masters. But his collecting fury was aroused by Far Eastern art. First, he concentrated upon Japanese wood-block prints and Japanese ceramics. He was happy and stimulated by every single acquisition, and there was no end to his desire—and energy—to discover all he could about the history and cultural significance of each piece, each artist, each period and each style.

Hans had the unusual gift of making friends with people from all walks of life, including artists and scholars of the highest order. He took and incorporated their observations into his own ever-widening and deepening appreciation of fine art. He became more and more interested in Chinese art. His great mentor and adviser in this field was Dr. Fujio Koyama of Tokyo with whom he developed a real friendship.

While Hans carried on his business, he could devote only a limited time to his collection, since he continued to be interested in music and literature, his circle of friends and, of course, his family. From the beginning, I took part in his artistic enterprise and assisted him with the cataloging and the display of the collection.

With the years it became increasingly difficult to display the collection, not only because of its growth in size and importance, but also because museums were increasingly aware of it and made numerous requests for loans. It was Hans' conviction that it was a collector's happy obligation to share his treasures with the interested public, and loans to museums were one way of achieving this.

When he retired in 1967, Hans was able to devote as much time as he wanted to art, and combined his vacation trips with bidding and purchasing arrangements wherever auctions and buying opportunities beckoned. His Chinese collection grew in quality and quantity, but unfortunately the cupboards in our home appeared to shrink. The playroom had to be sacrificed and converted into a display room. The design of this museum *en miniature* was determined to the minutest detail by Hans. It was touching to watch his joy and excitement as each piece found its place according to his loving and understanding mind and hand. He filled the years from 1967 until his untimely death in 1971 with his passion for Oriental art. The intensity of his dedication was felt by all who knew him and by the many visitors who were attracted not only by his collection, but also by his contagious enthusiasm.

I am very grateful to Professor Yvon d'Argencé, the Asian Art Commission of San Francisco and the staff of the Center of Asian Art and Culture for organizing the present exhibition.

Gretl Popper

Introduction

HANS and Gretl Popper began collecting assiduously and systematically about twenty years ago. Almost immediately they displayed an unusual taste for contemporary Western paintings, traditional African artifacts and Far Eastern *objects d'art*. The present catalogue is concerned exclusively with the Chinese and Korean sections of the collection.

It seems that at first Hans and Gretl Popper were mainly attracted by Japanese ceramics and prints which they acquired in large and important groups. However, with time, and under the guidance of such eminent specialists as Fujio Koyama, they became increasingly sensitive to the subtle quality of early Chinese Monochromes and Korean Celadons. An outstanding assemblage of such ceramics is accompanied in this exhibition by a choice series of ancient Chinese bronzes and another of early Buddhist sculptures. For all its variety, this selection, taken in its entirety, is the expression of an obvious predilection for robust architectural shapes, simple contours and warm but relatively unadorned surfaces.

The Chinese Bronze Age

China's first metallurgical experiments do not seem to have taken place much earlier than the middle of the second millennium B.C., but relatively late as they were in materializing, the esthetic and technical achievements of the Chinese Bronze Age surpassed those of any other part of the world. Drawing upon a very rich and diversified ceramic heritage, bronze casters of the Shang and Chou dynasties were able to produce an incredible number of highly original shapes and decorative motifs. The ritual vessels, which constitute their most sophisticated, best known and most sought after creations, are the results of somewhat erratic alloys and of multi-mold casting; a technique so elaborate that it continues to keep most of its secrets in the face of modern technology after two or three decades of intensive research.

Throughout the Bronze Age, which lasted until the end of the Warring States period or the beginning of the Han dynasty, bronze was a semi-precious material far too expensive to be of common use. It was accessible only to those in power, and they used it mainly for religious, ceremonial or military purposes. During the Shang and Early Western Chou period, vessels of the type illustrated in Nos. 1 to 6 served for the offering of wine and food to the spirits of ancestors and to the deities of a large pantheon that seems to have been the main source of inspiration for the decoration of the vessels themselves. Ablutionary vessels were also made but in lesser quantities. Sizes vary from containers so large that they had to be carried by several men, to diminutive ones that can be held in the palm of one's hand. Most, however, had approximately the same size as those illustrated here.

Starting with the Western Chou dynasty, owing to the establishment of new religious concepts and of a feudal society, there was a gradual change from strictly sacrificial vessels to more worldly ones that were made specifically to commemorate particularly important events, to reward special services, or more simply, to express consideration for a member of one's clan or family. This reorientation of the bronze industry is reflected by new shapes, new decorative themes and also new types of inscriptions, lengthier, more explicit and more factual.

Belt hooks and mirrors are among the most significant, elaborate and typical shapes of the Warring States and Western Han periods. Both these categories of objects are represented in the Popper collection by a number of carefully selected items (Nos. 11 to 19).

All the bronze vessels or artifacts included in this exhibition come from tombs where they remained for many a century. Through contact with earth chemicals, bronze alloys developed colorful patinae, the texture and abstract patterns of which are particularly valued by Western collectors, even though they played no part in the original make up of the objects.

Early Chinese Ceramics

The Popper collection contains more than ninety pieces of ceramics ranging from the Warring States period to the Yüan dynasty. This is by far the largest section in the collection, as it represents about two-thirds of the total number of items. White wares of the T'ang, Five Dynasties and Sung, numbering sixteen items, are of special interest at a time when various hypotheses regarding the origin of white porcelain in China are being reevaluated (Nos. 69 to 75 and 93 to 102).

By the end of the Warring States, Chinese potters were the heirs of a two thousand year-old tradition. During these two millennia of constant and painstaking research to refine their product, their predecessors had greatly improved their tools and technical skill. They knew how to select plastic clays, how to purify them and fire them in sophisticated kilns to stoneware hardness. In the Wu-Yüeh region, which played a major part in the development of Chinese ceramics, potters even knew how to make and apply glazes. Simultaneously, Chinese potters had developed a predilection for robust functional shapes and colorful surfaces.

Yet for all these technical achievements and consistency in aesthetic pursuits, the history of porcelain was still in its infancy. Many more centuries would elapse before all the material ingredients and calorific agents that go into the making of true porcelain could be fully mastered.

Throughout the Han and Six Dynasties the bulk of ceramic production consisted of unglazed, low-fired containers, human and animal statuettes, or architectural models, many of which were made specifically as tomb furniture (Nos. 36, 37, 40 and 45 to 47). Nevertheless, Han potters are to be credited with the invention of lead and feldspathic glazes which they colored with various oxides of metallic origin, mainly iron and copper (Nos. 38 and 39). Simultaneously, various kilns in the Wu-Yüeh region maintained their technical advance. The olive-green glazed stonewares which they produced toward the end of the Han dynasties and during the Six Dynasties are rightly, if rather awkwardly, known as proto-porcelains (Nos. 41 to 44).

The T'ang dynasty was a time of colorful splendor. An enthusiastic and occasionally clamorous taste for rich materials and bright pigments permeated all art media. This gave a new orientation to the ceramic research which became more and more involved in chromatic experiments. With a few exceptions, generally of foreign origin (No. 50), T'ang shapes are remarkably simple, matter-of-fact, functional. Not so with T'ang glazes, which display an astonishing array of hues and colors (Nos. 56 to 68), including some striking innovations (Nos. 58 to 60). Until quite recently, these opulent monochromes and so-called "three-colored" wares could be regarded as the main, if not exclusive, contribution of the T'ang period to the ceramic art of China, but during the past two decades or so, scholars and archaeologists have discovered a number of porcelaneous white wares which shed an entirely new light on the origin of white porcelain in China (Nos. 69 to 75). A great deal of research remains to be done before geographical, chronological and typological charts can be established, but there is no longer any doubt that true white porcelain was produced early in the T'ang dynasty, if not slightly earlier. Nor is there any reason to continue to ascribe all early white porcelains to Hsing-yao or even to Hopei province. Recent excavations of T'ang kilns in Honan, Kiangsi and even Szechwan have yielded large quantities of white porcelain sherds.

In the north, the Liao dynasty of Mongol origin prolonged T'ang tastes and attitudes well into the 12th century while introducing a few new nomadic shapes and techniques (Nos. 76 to 79). In the rest of the country, however, the turbulent, ephemeral Five Dynasties and the longer-lived, but fragile Sung dynasty marked the beginning of an entirely new ceramic era. Following a period of colorful exuberance and ebullient vitality, the Sung dynasty is an age of quiet introspection, with strong poetical and philosophical overtones. This mutation is particularly apparent in the field of ceramics. Opulent coloring is replaced by subtle glazes or surfaces painted, for the most part, with the parsimony that characterizes contemporaneous painting. The Sung dynasty is also an age of technical excellence. The ceramic art is reaching its apogee with a number of monochrome porcelains that have remained models of perfection until the present day and were imitated by imperial kilns as late as the 18th century. Such monochromes occupy a prominent place in the Popper collection. Practically all the main categories are abundantly represented: jade-like Northern (Nos. 83 to 87) and Southern Celadons (Nos. 88 to 92); silver-like, thin-bodied Ting wares (Nos. 98 to 102); dainty, blue-tinted Ch'ing-pai wares (Nos. 103 to 108); heavily potted, opalescent Chün-yao wares (Nos. 109 to 114); sturdy brown stonewares from Honan and Fukien (Nos. 115 to 123); and the elusive Kuan ware which many regard as the best porcelain ever made (Nos. 126 and 127).

Y. A.

11

1 *LI-TING*

Late Shang
13th to 11th century B.C.
Bronze
H. 8 in.   W. 7 in.   C-24

This three-lobed ceremonial food vessel stands on three solid cylindrical legs. The overhanging flaring mouth rim is topped by two sturdy loop handles, and the three lobes fuse into each other to form the body of the vessel.   All these structural features are typical of the *li-ting* class and are consequently rather commonplace.   Conversely, the decor of the vessel is most unusual, perhaps as much in the choice of the motifs as in their execution.   The lobes of most *li-ting* illustrate the same association of motifs, i.e. large *t'ao-t'ieh* masks flanked by vertical dragons. Here each mask is framed on either side by highly stylized birds which are so closely integrated in the mask that they can be interpreted as mere extensions of it. The neck-band, too, is atypical.   It is divided into six panels by short and shallow ridges.   Each panel contains an animal band which looks like a myriapod and multi-crested dragon, owing to the presence of numerous hooks above and below the elongated ribbon which takes the place of the dragon's body.   All panels are identical and are grouped two by two on the three axes which correspond to the depressions of the lobes.   When seen from that angle, the animal bands confront each other and form diminutive *t'ao-t'ieh* masks.

With the exception of the *t'ao-t'iehs'*, birds' and dragons' eyes, which stand out in high relief, all these motifs are rendered in a rare type of boldly spiraling incisions that produce a fully calligraphic effect and are enhanced by some sort of black filling.   Another interesting aspect of the decor rests with the presence of the many little barbs that accentuate the movement of the smaller spirals.

There is a four-character inscription cast inside the vessel.   It reads *K'ang Ts'e Fu I*, which could be translated: "K'ang being breveted [made this vessel] for Father I."[1]

The whole surface is covered with a smooth light-green patina with red and green encrustations.

(1) See Bernhard Karlgren, *A Catalogue of the Chinese Bronzes in the Alfred F. Pillsbury Collection*, Minneapolis 1953, p. 74, fig. 31.

2 *FANG I*

Late Shang
An-yang style (ca. 1300 to 1028 B.C.)
Bronze
H. 8 5/8 in.   W. 4 7/8 in.   C-36

A square, box-like vessel for sacrificial wine, this *fang i* has a roof-shaped cover topped by a knob that looks like a miniature of the cover.   The bottom of the body is on a level with the narrow and plain strip that separates the main band of decoration from the foot-band.   The base is hollow and perforated on each of the four sides with large semicircular notches.

Lid and body are divided into eight panels by narrow scored flanges which serve as axes for the decor.   Atypically, there are large, long-tailed confronting birds on the lid,[1] while confronting beaked dragons decorate both the upper and foot zones of the body.   The main zone on each side consists of a large shielded *t'ao-t'ieh* mask with lateral avian legs and dragon-shaped horns.   With the exceptions of the protruding eyes, all these motifs stand flat against a background of square meanders.   The knob of the lid is incised with an abbreviated and inverted *t'ao-t'ieh* mask.

A large character *ting* (used here as a generic term meaning sacrificial vessel) is cast on the base.

Both vessel and lid are covered with a smooth grey-green patina.

(1)   Many vessels of this type have been published, but to my knowledge none of them has this lid decoration which is therefore quite a unique feature.

3 KU

Later Part of Late Shang
11th century B.C.
Bronze
H. 12 ¹/₂ in.   W. 7 in.   C-3

A chalice-like goblet for drinking sacrificial wine, this *ku* has a widely flaring trumpet and a high-stepped foot.   Combined with the high-flanged and tubular receptacle, these features are typical of the last phase in the evolution of the *ku*, a category of vessels the casting of which was almost abruptly discontinued after the downfall of the Shang dynasty.

The trumpet is decorated with rising blades and the central and foot zones with dissolved *t'ao-t'ieh* masks standing in low relief against a background of square meanders.   Quite in keeping with the remarkably consistent iconography of this class of vessels, the two narrow collar zones above and below the central part show diminutive reptiles and dragons of the trunked type.   The base of the central zone exhibits two cruciform depressions.

Cast in the hollow foot is an inscription of two graphs including a chariot[1] and the character for "arm-pit" (*i*).[2]

The patina is greenish-grey with malachite encrustations.

(1) For a similar vessel and a comparable graph of a chariot, see John Alexander Pope et al., *The Freer Chinese Bronzes*, Vol. I, Washington 1967, Number Nine, Pl. 9 and p. 67.

(2) The meaning of this inscription remains obscure, as pointed out by Dr. Noel Barnard in John Alexander Pope et al., *op. cit.* p. 345.

4 TSUN
Late Shang or Early Western Chou
11th to 10th century B.C.
Bronze
H. 9 5/8 in. Diam. at mouth. 7 1/2 in.   *C-26*

The trumpet and foot of this stocky beaker-like wine vessel are plain with the exception of a couple of "bowstrings" located on either side of the central zone. The latter is decorated with two large shielded *t'ao-t'ieh* masks that stand in high relief against a meander background. The masks are flanked by abbreviated vertical dragons in lower relief.[1]

A large graph depicting a hand holding an arrow is cast inside the foot.[2]

The smooth grey patination displays a few patches of thin malachite.

(1) A group of similar vessels has been published by Umehara Sueji in *Shina Kodō Seika*, Vol. II, Osaka 1960, Pls. 149, 150 and 151.

(2) Cf. Lo Chen-yü, *Chen Sung T'ang Chi Ku I Wen*, Vol. 4, Chang-chou 1931, p. 22-b.

5 *KUEI*
Early Western Chou
10th century B.C.
Bronze
H. 6 $^5/_{16}$ in.   Diam. at mouth 7 $^1/_4$ in.   C-1

This ceremonial food vessel has a somewhat bristling appearance which is due partly to the angular silhouette of its oversized handles, partly to the spiky flanges that jut out from various parts of its body and foot, and partly to some elements of the decor that project out from the surface of the vessel in an almost aggressive manner.[1]

The ornamentation of the body consists of large confronted, coil-bodied dragons that fill almost all of the available space and stand out in high relief against a meander background.   Their trunked mouths are gaping and reveal a pair of conical fangs.   Hook-shaped crests jut out vertically from the dome of their heads.   Their taloned legs are those of birds of prey.   The narrow foot zone is divided into four panels by short hooked flanges.   Each panel contains a pair of S-shaped, goggle-eyed snakes.   The massive, composite loop handles represent bovine heads holding a bird in their mouths.   The birds are largely conventionalized with the exception of free-sculpted beaks and also of talons and tail-feathers that stand out in relief on the spurs of the handles.

A three-column, fourteen-character inscription is engraved into the vessel on the bottom and reads: "The marquis made for Lady [unidentified graph] Mu [this] honored sacrificial vessel.   May it be treasured and used for a myriad years and forever."

The patina is black and silvery with green patches.

(1) Published: Tokyo Imperial Household Museum, *Relics of Han and Pre-Han Dynasties; Catalogue of the Exhibition Held in May 1932*, [in] *the Imperial Household Museum*, Tokyo 1932, Pl. XVII. For similar vessels, see also Sueji Umehara, *Selected Relics of Ancient Chinese Bronzes from Collections in Japan*, Vol. II, Osaka 1940, Pl. 106-B; Max Loehr, *Relics of Ancient China from the Collection of Dr. Paul Singer*, The Asia Society, Inc., [New York 1965], Pl. 40; and Ko Chin, "Ching-yang Kao-chia-pao Tsao Chou Mu Tsang Fa-chüeh Chi," *Wen Wu*, No. 7, 1972, pp. 5–8 and 67, fig. 3 recording an excavation that took place in the winter of 1971.

6 YU

Early Western Chou
10th century B.C.
Bronze
H: 11 ¹/₄ in.   *C-27*

This bucket-like vessel was used for holding ceremonial wine. It has an oval section, a massive bow-shaped swing handle that spans the wider axis, and a close-fitting, domed lid with a bud-like knob formed by four animal masks in relief.

The vessel is decorated only sparingly on the lid, shoulder and foot. The narrow band of decoration on the lid consists of eight groups of two gaping dragons with hooked crests and dissolved bodies. These dragons stand out in thick raised lines against a plain background. This band is framed by two "bowstrings" above and one below. The shoulder band is identical with the one that has just been described with two exceptions: the disposition of the framing "bowstrings" is reversed, and the central shielded ridges are replaced by ovine heads in high relief. The foot-band is reduced to a couple of "bowstrings."

The handle is decorated with four elongated dragons in low relief and terminate in free-sculptured bovine heads with "bottle" horns. [1]

Two 3-character identical inscriptions are cast inside the cover and on the base of the vessel. The first character, a pictogram, depicts an animal, possibly a deer or a dog. The other two read "Father Chi." [2]

The somewhat pitted and porous surface of the vessel is covered with a pale green patina with brownish and malachite markings.

(1)   This vessel belongs to a well-known type. See, for instance, William Watson, *Ancient Chinese Bronzes*, London 1962, Pl. 16, for a comparable example.
(2)   Compare inscription in John Alexander Pope et al., *The Freer Chinese Bronzes*, Vol. 1, Washington 1967, p. 313. See also Liu T'i-chih, compiler, *Hsiao Chiao Ching Ko Chin Shih Wen Tzu*, Vol. 4, [n.p., Pref. 1935], p. 22.

7 TSENG

Late Ch'un-ch'iu or Early Warring States
6th to 5th century B.C.
Bronze
H. 6 ¹/₂ in.   C-25

This large bowl-like container with high S-shaped handles, slightly constricted neck and perforated bottom is the upper part of a *hsien*, a steamer vessel used for the cooking of sacrificial and ceremonial food.   As clearly indicated by three vertical and one horizontal seams, the bowl proper was cast from six piece-molds. From under the flat overhanging mouth rim to about the middle of the body, the vessel is decorated with four horizontal bands of stamped motifs.   Three of these bands consist of a close-knit pattern of vermiculous shapes that can be reduced to a single unit, a pair of hook-beaked, half-bird, half-snake creatures.   These hybrids face one another and are placed top to bottom.   The lowermost band is made of a row of hanging blades inscribed with *t'ao-t'ieh* masks. [1]

(1)   For a similar vessel, complete with the *li* part, see René-Yvon Lefebvre d'Argencé, "The Magic World of the Chinese Bronze [in the Avery Brundage Collection]," *Apollo*, Vol. LXXXIV, No. 54, August 1966, p. 123, fig. 15.

8 TRIPOD

Warring States
5th to 3rd century B.C.
Bronze
H. 4 ¹/₂ in.   C-28

This unusual cup-shaped vessel stands on three minute baluster legs.   Two *t'ao-t'ieh* masks are placed high on the waist of the vessel.   They held ring handles that are now missing.   A series of twelve triangular and pointed hanging blades cover the upper and middle parts of the vessel.   Finely incised, they contain highly stylized and curvilinear *t'ao-t'ieh* motifs which recall the masks and dragons of earlier times.   The smooth patination is grey-green with patches of azurite. [1]

(1)   A taller, but comparable vessel was recently found in a Warring States tomb at Liu-ch'eng-ch'iao near Ch'ang-sha; see Wen-wu Ch'u-pan-she, *Wen-hua Ta Ke-ming Ch'i-chien Ch'u-t'u Wen-wu*, Vol. 1, Peking 1972, Pl. 35.

9 FANG-HU
Western Han
2nd to 1st century B.C.
Bronze
H. 6 ³/₄ in.   *C-38*

The body of this small vessel is plain with the exception of two *t'ao-t'ieh* masks that hold torquated ring handles. At the apex of the pyramidal lid a similar handle occupies the center of a square panel decorated with a quatrefoil and four minute circles. This panel is surrounded by a band of highly stylized dragons. The brown-grey patina is marked with heavy patches of reddish encrustations.

10 LIEN
Han
206 B.C. *to 221* A.D.
Gilt bronze
Diam. 5 in.   *C-29*

This small cylindrical box standing on three feet was probably used to keep cosmetics. The lid is missing. The central zone of decoration consists of a sunken band incised with floral and geometric patterns. Four feline masks set symmetrically on the upper part of the band used to hold rings which are missing. The feet are in the shape of squatting bears.

Some of the gilding has disappeared to be replaced by patches of green patina with malachite and azurite encrustations.

11 BELT HOOK

Warring States
4th or 3rd century B.C.
Bronze with gold inlays
L. 2 1/2 in.   *C-20*

The fan-shaped body of this bird or snake derivation is covered with a rich pattern of volutes arranged symmetrically. A similar piece was excavated recently at Hou-ma-ch'iao, near Ch'ü-wu in Shansi.[1]

(1) Published in Wen-wu Ch'u-pan-she, *Wen-hua Ta Ke-ming Ch'i-chien Ch'u-t'u Wen-wu*, Vol. I, Peking 1972, p. 138.

12 BELT HOOK

Warring States
4th or 3rd century B.C.
Bronze with gold and turquoise inlays
L. 8 1/4 in.   *C-21*

The faceted body is heavily adorned with a geometrical pattern consisting essentially of spirals and volute-and-angle figures. The hook resembles the head of a snake or a dragon.[1]

(1) For similar objects, see for instance Jean-Pierre Dubosc, *Exhibition of Chinese Art*, Venice 1954, fig. 113; and Bernhard Karlgren, "Chinese Agraffes in Two Swedish Collections," *BMFEA*, No. 38, Stockholm 1966, Pl. 29.

13 BELT HOOK

Warring States
4th or 3rd century B.C.
Bronze with silver inlays
L. 4 1/8 in.   *C-22*

The short, slightly arched and rounded body and the neck of this belt hook are covered with an intricate design of spirals of various sizes. The main spirals are filled with little dots suggesting matting and form a loose 8-shape. In his description of two similar objects in the collection of Dr. Paul Singer,[1] Max Loehr suggested that the design might represent a transformed bird figure. The head, which seems to be that of a dragon, is decorated with a geometrical pattern.

(1) Max Loehr, *Relics of Ancient China from the Collection of Dr. Paul Singer*, The Asia Society, Inc. [New York 1965], p. 159, nos. 90 and 91.

14 FRAGMENT OF A BELT HOOK

Warring States
4th or 3rd century B.C.
Gilt bronze
W. 1 1/2 in.   C-15

This is the top part of a belt hook.   Originally the animal formed a large 8-shaped loop and was biting its own spine.   The lower part of the body and the hook are now missing.[1]   The gilding has almost entirely disappeared; the brown patina has malachite encrustations.

(1)   See Bernhard Karlgren, "Chinese Agraffes in Two Swedish Collections," *BMFEA*, No. 38, Stockholm 1966, Pl. 61, 07W for a similar and complete item.

15 BELT HOOK

Warring States
Ca. 3rd century B.C. *Possibly from Shou-chou.*
Bronze
L. 3 3/8 in.   C-12

The relatively small body resembles the head of an animal of the fox family.   This head consists of two triangular ears, two socketed eyes which were probably inlaid with semi-precious stones, now missing, a beak-like nose and a granulated face traversed longitudinally by a central stripe.   The neck and hook part of this object are of crude workmanship.[1]

(1)   Compare with Alfred Salmony, *Sino-Siberian Art in the Collection of C. T. Loo*, Paris 1933, Pl. XX, fig. 1; Nils Palmgren, *Selected Chinese Antiquities from the Collection of Gustaf Adolf, Crown Prince of Sweden*, Stockholm 1948, Pl. 32, fig. 10; and Bernhard Karlgren, "Chinese Agraffes in Two Swedish Collections," *BMFEA*, No. 38, Stockholm 1966, Pl. 77, R4W.

16 BELT HOOK

Probably Han
3rd century B.C. *to 3rd century* A.D.
Ordos style
Bronze
L. 3 in.   K-11

The horse, shown in suspended motion, has a powerful arched neck, a small triangular head and a stumpy, hook-shaped tail.   The animal is directed toward the hook which projects out from the front leg.   From the other side, which is concave, protrudes a squarish knob with a short cylindrical shank.[1]   The patina is light green and fairly smooth.

(1)   A very similar item is published in Bernhard Karlgren, "Chinese Agraffes in Two Swedish Collections," *BMFEA*, No. 38, Stockholm 1966, Pl. 68, P11W.

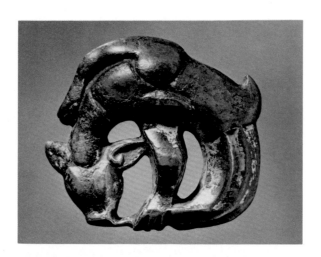

17 *MIRROR OF THE SHOU-CHOU TYPE*

Late Warring States
3rd century B.C.
Bronze
Diam. 4 1/2 in.   *C-30*

The main decor of this thin, circular mirror with an elevated rim and a fluted central loop consists of a dense interlacing of three dragon figures. Treated like spiraling ribbons, these figures are so dissolved, abstracted and distorted that they have lost most of their naturalistic features. These motifs stand in flat relief against a granulated background with geometrical schemes in raised lines. The loop occupies the center of a small circular panel surrounded by two narrow concentric bands with striations forming a herringbone pattern. A third narrow band, also striated, separates the main zone from the rim.[1] The patina is smooth and black, with a few jade-like light green markings.

(1) A very similar object is published by Bernhard Karlgren in his "Huai and Han," *BMFEA*, No. 13, Stockholm 1941, Pl. 45, E28 and is said to have come from Shou-chou in Anhui province.

18   *MIRROR OF DRAGON-TIGER TYPE*

Eastern Han
25 B.C. *to 221* A.D.
Bronze
Diam. 4 ³/₈ in.   *C-34*

The central panel is also the main field of decoration.   It contains a large, sturdy knob surrounded by a dragon and a tiger whose contorted bodies are so arranged that they fill the panel and take the form of its circular contour.   These animals stand in high relief against a background of raised lines and spirals.   The rest of the ornamentation consists of five concentric bands.   One is plain, while the others illustrate various geometric patterns.   The pale grey patina contains large areas of green discoloration. [1]

(1)   A large number of similar mirrors have been excavated in Chekiang province; see for instance Wang Shih-lun, *Che-chiang Ch'u-t'u T'ung Ching Hsüan-chi*, Peking 1957, Pl. 36 and ff.

19   *MIRROR WITH PICTORIAL DECORATION*

Late Eastern Han or Early Six Dynasties
3rd century A.D.
Bronze
Diam. 4 ⁵/₁₆ in.   *C-33*

The center field of this mirror consists of a hemispherical knob (now slightly out of shape) and of a circular panel with deities, mythical beasts and crested birds. The panel is surrounded by a band of twelve circular lobes alternating with twelve squares.   Both squares and lobes are in fairly high relief.   The former stand out against a granulated background, the latter partly against the same background and partly against sections of a band of semicircles.   The squares enclose a dedicatory inscription which is partly obliterated.   The next band is decorated with a sawtooth pattern, and the next one bears another dedicatory inscription in raised lines and also partly obliterated.   The outer band consists of a zigzagging line with spiraling barbs. [1]

(1)   For comparable mirrors see Sueji Umehara, *Selected Ancient Mirrors Found at Shao-hsing Tombs*, Kyoto 1939, Pls. 4 and 5.

20 LINCHPIN
Late Shang
13th to 11th century B.C.
Bronze
L. 4 in.   C-10

The head of this sturdy linchpin is in the shape of a half cylinder and shows a *t'ao-t'ieh* mask in fairly high relief.   The mouthless and chinless monster has a sensitive realistic muzzle, two large bulging eyes and C-shaped horns.   The overhanging semicircular top of the head looks like a flat headgear. A large perforation, located behind the horns, runs through the entire width of the head.   The patina is greyish-green with lighter green and red encrustations.

21 HANDLE
Warring States
5th to 3rd century B.C.
Bronze
H. 4 1/4 in.   C-8

The handle, which may be that of a ceremonial staff or weapon, is surmounted by a human head with mongoloid features that are accentuated to the point of being caricatural.   The brown patina is heavily encrusted with red and green patches.

22 TIGER
Warring States
Ca. 3rd century B.C.
Bronze
L. 4 1/8 in.   C-35

The lithe animal has an arched, hollow body, a long spiraling tail and short sturdy legs.   The head is turned all the way back, and the toothless mouth is wide open. Body and tail are incised with "triangle and spiral" motifs, and the neck is scaled. The shoulders and haunches are marked with studs and comma-shaped loops. The feet are perforated with fairly large attachment holes.   This feature, added to the form of the body and the attitude of the animal, indicates that it must have served as the handle of a vessel.[1] The patination is dark green.

(1)   See for instance W. Perceval Yetts, *The Cull Chinese Bronzes*, London 1939, Pl. XVII.

23 *ORNAMENTAL PLAQUE*

Ordos
4th to 3rd century B.C.
Bronze
L. 2 ¹/₄ in.   C-14

The plaque is rectangular with a double rope border forming a loose chevron pattern.   One of the small sides has a projection in its middle and is perforated with a suspension hole.   The entire field is filled with a yak shown in profile with its head turned to one side.[1]   All the decor is done in shallow relief.   The patina is brownish and contains green encrustations.

(1)   For similar items, see Mikhail I. Rostovtsev, *The Animal Style in South Russia and China*, Princeton 1929, Pl. XXVII, figs. 2 and 4; and Karl Jettmar, *Art of the Steppes*, New York 1967, p. 159 (top left).

24 *CHAIN HOLDER*

Ordos
4th to 3rd century B.C.
Bronze
L. 1 ¹/₂ in.   C-16

The chain holder is in the shape of a tiger shown in profile and standing on two large rings to which the chain was attached.   Details are blurred owing to heavy corrosion, but some features are still discernible, such as the stripes of the fur which are rendered by incisions, and the claws which take the form of small circles.   The back is concave and is equipped with two small attachment loops.[1]   The original patina is dark brown, and small patches of an artificial green patina have been added.

(1)   For a similar item, see Alfred Salmony, *Sino-Siberian Art in the Collection of C. T. Loo*, Paris 1933, Pl. XXXII, fig. 1.

25   YA-SHENG CH'IEN (?)

Han
206 B.C. *to 221* A.D.
Bronze
H. 6 ⁷/₈ in.   *C-19*

This coin to ward off evil influence (?) (*Ya-sheng ch'ien*) is made of an elaborate handle and a rectangular plaque both in openwork.   The shape is derived from that of a sword or long knife with a pommel, a handle and a blade.[1]   What was originally a ring pommel has taken the shape of a twisting snake.   The shaft of the handle consists of a winged horse enclosed in a square frame.   The blade (or plaque) is decorated with a peculiar dragon design covered with innumerable asperities recalling granulation work.   Both sides of the piece are identical.   The patination is evenly green.

(1)   See *Catalogue of the International Exhibition of Chinese Art, 1935–36*, London 1936, where a similar object (fig. 562) is described as a charm; and Cheng Te-k'un, *Archaeological Studies in Szechwan*, Cambridge 1957, Pl. 67, figs. 1 and 2 for an almost identical piece and other examples in the same series. See also Paul Singer, "Some Puzzle Pieces," *Oriental Art*, Vol. XVIII, No. 2, Summer 1972, pp. 155–162, figs. 6, 7, 8 and 9. Dr. Singer does not seem to accept either identification and would like to leave the question open.

26   STAFF FINIAL
Han
206 B.C. *to 221* A.D.
Bronze
L. 4 ¹/₈ in.   *C-9*

This finial consists of the head and part of the neck of a goose.   The lower part of the hollow neck—now missing—was perforated with two attachment holes. The heavily encrusted patina is green.

(1)   There is a similar and complete finial in the Avery Brundage Collection (B60 B839).

27   STAFF FINIAL
Han
206 B.C. *to 221* A.D.
Bronze
H. 3 ¹/₈ in.   *C-11*

This finial consists of the head and neck of a bird.   The head proper is small, but is equipped with a prominent crest and a curved beak of inordinate proportions. The hollow neck served as a socket and is perforated with two attachment holes. There is an earlier and more elaborate specimen of this type of finial in the collection of the King of Sweden.[1]   The reddish-brown patina is encrusted with green patches.

(1)   See Bo Gyllensvärd and John Alexander Pope, *Chinese Art from the Collection of H. M. King Gustaf VI Adolph of Sweden*, New York 1966, p. 37, fig. 34.

28   WEIGHT (?) IN THE SHAPE OF A WINGED TIGER
Six Dynasties
Ca. 3rd century A.D.
Bronze with gold inlays
H. 2 ⁵/₈ in.   *C-7*

The beast stands on its splayed legs in an attitude of suspended motion, with its head raised and turned to one side.   The growling mouth is open and shows bare teeth and fangs.   Details of the goatee, spine, neck, wings, tail and legs are rendered in thin threads of gold.[1]

(1)   For a comparable item, see Jean-Pierre Dubosc, *Exhibition of Chinese Art*, Venice 1954, p. 55, no. 160.

29   *BUST OF BODHISATTVA*

Northern Wei
First part of the 6th century A.D.
Probably from Lung-men, Honan
Limestone, H. 12 ³/₈ in.   *C-101*

This is a fragment of a full-length relief that was cut directly from the wall of
a cave-temple.   The meditating Bodhisattva holds his head slightly inclined to
the right with his chin resting on the tips of the fingers of his right hand.   He
wears a high flaring tiara.   The face is elongated, the crescent-shaped eyes are
closed, and a faint smile hovers over the full, slightly pouting lips.   The wing-like
ears cover the entire span of the head.[1]

(1)   Published: Langdon Warner, *Pacific Cultures*, San Francisco 1939, Pl. G, fig. 69.

30 *SEATED BUDDHA*
Six Dynasties
5th century A.D.
Gilt bronze
H. 3 ¹/₂ in.   *C-116*

This statuette ranks among the earliest representations of the Buddha made by Chinese sculptors. Like all such early effigies, it retains a good deal of Gandharan influence.[1] This influence is particularly manifest in the posture and type of garment.[2]

The Buddha is seated in meditation on a squarish, bulky lion throne. His head and body are bent gently forward, and his hands rest on his lap, all finger tips in contact with one another. The head and hands are very large, and the legs are extremely elongated. Conversely, the almost semicircular torso is rather squat. All this is very much in keeping with archaic iconographical tendencies. The rounded face with bold, if somewhat blunt features bears a benign, half-smiling expression. With the exception of a few incisions over the forehead, the hair is plain and sleek. It covers an unusually large cranial protruberance (*uṣṇīṣa*). The body is practically hidden under the heavy robe which falls in cascading folds, forming a kind of flat apron in front. Only the forepart of the lions, which stand on either side of the throne, is visible. The lions are represented in a stiff, frontal and menacing posture. The central field of the throne between the lions is decorated with an incised design which is not easily identifiable, but might represent a lappet with tassels, probably suggesting a section of the cloth which was spread over the throne. The front of the base of the throne or the platform on which it is place is incised with wavy lines. Similar lines decorate the semicircular area that extends from the neck to the shoulders and looks like a misinterpretation of the typical Gandharan "rolled" collar.

Both statuette and pedestal are hollow. A perforated tenon projects from the back of the head. It was used for supporting a now-missing halo.[3]

(1) See for instance René-Yvon Lefebvre d'Argencé, *Chinese Treasures from the Avery Brundage Collection*, The Asia Society, Inc., New York 1968, frontispiece.

(2) Compare with Benjamin Rowland, Jr., *The Evolution of the Buddha Image*, The Asia Society, Inc., New York 1963, Pl. 3.

(3) See Saburō Matsubara, *Chinese Buddhist Sculpture*, Tokyo 1966, Pl. 8-a for a very similar statuette.

31 *STANDING BODHISATTVA*

Eastern Wei
Dated 538 A.D.
Gilt bronze
H. 6 1/2 in.   *C-117*

This small, rather ill-shaped statuette rests on a hemispherical lotus pedestal supported by a high dais with splayed legs and stands in high relief against a large, leaf-shaped nimbus. With the exception of the feet and the stunted arms, the entire body is covered by a heavy robe and scarves. The folds of the robe are rendered in simple incised lines, and the scarves form winglike, pointed projections. The face of the nimbus is engraved with a lotus halo for the head, a plain body halo and a wide border of conventionalized flames.[1] All the components of this small shrine seem to have been cast in one piece. The rear part of the dais bears an incised inscription which reads: "In the first year of Yüan-hsiang[2] on the 16th day of the 5th month, Kuo T'ung-chou reverently made the Bodhisattva effigy. May the orthodox[3] law prevail where he [Kuo] was born and has been living. So does he wish."

(1) For a similar nimbus, see Saburō Matsubara, *Chinese Buddhist Sculpture*, Tokyo 1966, Pl. 121-d.
(2) The first year of Yüan-hsiang of the Eastern Wei dynasty corresponds to 538 A.D.
(3) The style of this character is a clear indication that the inscription—crude as it is—dates from the period in question.

32 *KUAN YIN*

T'ang
Late 7th to early 8th century A.D.
Gilt bronze
H. 9 1/4 in.   *C-118*

The Bodhisattva stands on a lotus pedestal in a graceful swaying pose with his left hip thrust out. The body is slender, and the limbs are elongated, particularly the sinuous, serpentine arms. The right hand holds a vase from which a lotus flower, now broken, arose; the left hand nonchalantly holds a willow spray. The lower part of the body from waist to ankles is covered with a *dhotī*-type skirt which clings to the legs. The bare torso is heavily adorned with flowing scarves and jewelry. The elaborate headdress, with flaring wings at the sides and a high topknot, includes a diminutive effigy of a seated Amitābha, Kuan Yin's spiritual father.[1] As it is usually the case in this series of statuettes, the face is unexpectedly full and fleshy. It is a vivid illustration of the self contentment that permeates so many High T'ang images. The hollow pedestal was badly damaged and was skillfully, if not entirely satisfactorily, reshaped. A perforated tenon projects from the flattened back of the statuette and served to secure a now-missing halo.

(1) For a similar and more complete piece, see René-Yvon Lefebvre d'Argencé, *Chinese Treasures from the Avery Brundage Collection*, The Asia Society, Inc., New York 1968, fig. 105.

33 *SEATED LION*

T'ang
Ca. 8th century A.D.
Gilt bronze
H. 1 ³/₄ in.   *C-139B*

This slender-waisted, fish-tailed lion was originally part of an altarpiece.[1] All head and limbs, it has a body which is reduced to a minimum. Its left paw is raised in a supposedly menacing gesture. This lithe, dynamic beast is to the one illustrated in No. 33 of this catalogue what some slender, graceful T'ang female figurines are to the contemporary series of plump ladies.[2]

(1) As clearly indicated by the presence of a long pin that projects from the underside of the animal.

(2) See René-Yvon Lefebvre d'Argencé, *Chinese Ceramics in the Avery Brundage Collection*, San Francisco 1967, p. 54.

34 *SEATED LION*

T'ang
Ca. 8th century A.D.
Gilt bronze
H. 1 ¹/₄ in.   *C-139A*

The squat, heavily corroded, yet lively animal is seated on a thick round slab with its left paw raised in mid-air. The body is lumped together, but the various components of the ferocious head are depicted in great detail.[1]

(1) This item closely resembles the pottery lion illustrated in No. 55 of this catalogue.

35 *SEATED BODHISATTVA (ĀKĀŚAGARBHA?)*
T'ang
Mid 8th to early 10th century A.D.
Gilt bronze
H. 5 3/4 in.   *C-119*

Seated in *padmāsana* on a high lotus pedestal, this Bodhisattva of esoteric Buddhism holds in his left hand the *cintāmaṇi* or sacred jewel, while the left hand makes a gesture of appeasement.[1]   The lower part of the body is covered with a *dhotī*-type skirt forming a series of ridge-like folds about the thighs and shins.   The bare torso is adorned with flowing streamers and jewelry including armlets and bracelets.   The streamers are, in fact, part of a very elaborate headdress, the most conspicuous element of which is a high crown made of floral scrolls and adorned in front with a jewel-like ornament.   Part of the hair, which is arranged in a high topknot, flows over the shoulders in well-defined, plaited strands.   The face has a slightly haughty and disillusioned expression that one finds in many late T'ang effigies.[2]   The upper part of the pedestal consists of three rows of strongly modeled lotus petals with incised decoration.   The lower part of the pedestal is made of four concentric tiers: first, a row of lotus petals, then two circles with foliate borders, and finally a round, six-lobed base.   A perforated tenon projects from the fully-modeled back of the statuette and was used to secure a now-missing halo.   This type of statuette can be regarded as the prototype of a large number of esoteric images made in Japan during the Heian period.[3]

(1) Published: Saburō Matsubara, *Chinese Buddhist Sculpture*, Tokyo 1966, Pl. 296.
(2) For another statuette in the same style and workmanship, see Henry Trubner, *The Arts of the T'ang Dynasty*, Los Angeles 1957, fig. 82.
(3) See for instance, Bunkazaihogoiinkai, *Kokuhō Jiten*, Tokyo 1961, p. 11 (Kokūzō Bosatsu-zō).

36 TING

Late Warring States or Western Han[1]
3rd to 1st century B.C.
Painted pottery
H. 5 3/4 in.   Diam. 7 1/2 in.   *C-5*

Made specifically to be buried with a dead person as part of the tomb furniture, this tripod was fashioned in the shape of a bronze *ting*.[2]   The massive globular body stands on three short baluster legs.   The two large L-shaped handles rise vertically above the mouth rim.   The vessel is of dark grey pottery.   The decoration that was painted in white, green, brown and purple is particularly elaborate. It is well-preserved on the cover where it consists of a quatrefoil surrounded by scrolls of spiraling clouds.

(1)   See also the frontispiece of this catalogue for another view of this tripod.
(2)   For a similar piece, see Robert L. Hobson, *The Eumorfopoulos Collection*, Vol. 1, London 1925, Pl. XVI, 94.

37 *HORSE'S HEAD*

Late Warring States or Western Han
3rd to 1st century B.C.
Painted pottery
H. 6 ⁵/₈ in.   *C-6*

The sharp angle that this nervous, bony and elongated head forms with the sturdy, vertical neck is typical of the period.   Holes placed high on the head once served to secure detachable ears which may have been made in a different material. Other holes on each side of the mouth were utilized for the insertion of a bit.   Both the head and neck are hollow, but partly filled with clay; made of grey pottery covered with red pigment, they still bear traces of the white paint which was used to indicate various parts of the harness.   This head is very similar to that of the well-known wooden horse in the Paul Singer Collection; the latter is thought to have been found in Ch'ang-sha and is consequently ascribed to the end of the Chou period.[1]

(1)   Max Loehr, *Relics of Ancient China from the Collection of Dr. Paul Singer*, The Asia Society, Inc., [New York 1965], Pl. 132 and jacket. See also Robert L. Hobson, *The Eumorfopoulos Collection*, Vol. 1, London 1925, Pl. XXI, 126; and *Catalogue of the Archaeological Collection in the Museum of the Faculty of Letters, Kyoto University*, Part 3, Kyoto 1963, p. 84, fig. 326.

38   *LADLE*

Han
206 B.C. *to 221* A.D.
Pottery with iridescent green glaze
L. 5 ³/₈ in.   *C-37*

This ladle, made to be buried with a deceased person as part of his tomb furniture, was modeled after a bronze prototype which served for measuring. [1]   It consists of a hemispherical bowl-like container and a handle in the shape of a long-necked dragon holding a pearl in its mouth. [2]   The bowl is decorated with a sawtooth pattern below the rim and barbed elongated scrolls all around the central register. The neck is adorned with rectangular cartouches enclosing geometrical designs. All these motifs are in raised lines.

(1)   Max Loehr, *Relics of Ancient China from the Collection of Dr. Paul Singer*, The Asia Society, Inc., [New York 1965], Pl. 123.
(2)   For similar examples, see *Sekai Tōji Zenshū*, Vol. 8, Tokyo 1955, Pl. 73; and Ireneus László Legeza, *A Descriptive and Illustrated Catalogue of the Malcolm MacDonald Collection of Chinese Ceramics*, London 1972, Pl. III, no. 7.

39   *HILL JAR*

Han
206 B.C. *to 221* A.D.
Pottery with iridescent green glaze
H. 6 ¹/₂ in.   Diam. 8 ³/₄ in.   *C-31*

The shape of this funerary cylindrical tripod is derived from a bronze prototype of the *lien* series. [1]   The animal feet, representing diminutive bears, are typical of the series.   So is the circular band framed at the top and bottom by a couple of "bowstrings."   This band illustrates in relief a mythical hunting scene with a variety of wild animals, including tigers and deer, and a mounted hunter.   Most of the animals are depicted in full gallop in a setting of wavy mountains.   The now-missing lid probably exhibited the usual molded rendering of Mount P'eng Lai, the Great Central Mountain of the Taoist Paradise. [2]   The base is unglazed and reveals a reddish body.

(1)   See for instance No. 10 in this catalogue.
(2)   Robert Treat Paine, Jr. in *The Charles B. Hoyt Collection Memorial Exhibition, February 13-March 30, 1952*, Boston [1952], fig. 52 illustrates a similar jar complete with cover. See also *Sekai Tōji Zenshū*, Vol. 8, Tokyo 1955, Pl. 1.

40 *FABULOUS BEAST*

Eastern Han
1st to 3rd century A.D.
Painted pottery
L. 12 in.   *C-32*

Part of tomb furnishings, this massive, short-legged, long-tailed animal with three spiky horns and stud-like vertebrae is sometimes likened to a rhinoceros,[1] an analogy which anatomists would hardly sanction.   It belongs to a numerous series of Han and Six Dynasties hybrids which still await proper identification.   The cylindrical protuberances located below the ears are vestiges of wings which are now missing.   In places, the dark grey body still shows traces of a white slip and of red pigments.   The finger-like horns and tail are replacements.   The body is hollow with a large rectangular aperture under the belly.

(1)   See for instance Robert L. Hobson, *The Eumorfopoulos Collection*, Vol. I, London 1925, Pl. XVII, 128; Satō Masahiko, *Chūgoku no Dogū*, Tokyo 1965, fig. 58; and *Sekai Bijutsu Zenshū*, Vol. 13, *Chūgoku*, Part 2, Tokyo 1962, fig. 123.

41 JAR

Eastern Han
1st to 3rd century A.D.
Stoneware with ash glaze, Yüeh-yao type
H. 12 in.   *C-4*

Neither the olive-green glaze nor the decoration extend to the plain reddish-brown lower part of this globular jar. Below the small everted mouth rim the upper part is divided by concentric grooved ridges into three bands. Two of these bands are incised with birdicized clouds. Two large *t'ao-t'ieh* handles are placed very high on the shoulder. Immediately above them two other monster masks stand out in low relief.[1]

(1) Similar jars were published in Robert Treat Paine, Jr., *The Charles B. Hoyt Collection Memorial Exhibition, February 13-March 30, 1952*, Boston [1952], fig. 62, and in *Sekai Kokōgaku Taikei*, Vol. 7, *Tō-Asia*, Part III, Tokyo 1963, fig. 45.

42   CHICKEN JAR
Western Chin or Wu
3rd to 4th century A.D.
Stoneware, Yüeh-yao
Diam. 5 1/4 in.   *C-138A*

The shoulder of this small globular jar is adorned with a bird's head on one side and the tip of a tail on the other.   The bird's head is fully modeled, with its beak slightly opened.   It serves as a spout since it communicates with the inside of the vessel.   Two large loop handles are set slightly lower on the shoulder and in axial position.   These handles are incised with a variant of the usual herringbone pattern while the upper part of the vessel and the small hat-like stopper are incised with bands of floral scrolls and parallel lines.   The grey body is entirely covered with an olive-green glaze, and there are five gritty kiln marks on the flat base.[1]

(1)   For comparable examples, see Chiang Hsüan-tai and Ch'in T'ing-yü, *Chung-kuo Tz'u-ch'i te Fa-ming*, Shanghai 1956, Pls. 17, 18 and 23.

43   EWER
Six Dynasties
3rd to 4th century A.D.
Stoneware, Yüeh-yao
L. 10 in.   *C-125*

The body of this zoomorphic ewer seems to be made of three jars fused into one another; two of comparable sizes and joined at the mouths for the body proper, and another one, smaller, for the head.   Since the upper part of this small jar is decorated in low relief with the mask of a lion, and since the body rests on four diminutive paws, this curious assemblage of abstract and realistic features constitutes a very convincing and humorous allusion to a crouching lion with a raised head and a gaping mouth.[1]   A bow handle links the back of the head to the rump of the animal and is incised with a rope pattern.   Except for the flat rear, which can serve as an alternate base, the buff body is covered with a greyish-green glaze.

(1)   For similar examples, see Robert Treat Paine, Jr., *The Charles B. Hoyt Collection Memorial Exhibition, February 13-March 30, 1952*, Boston [1952], fig. 212; and *Sekai Kokōgaku Taikei*, Vol. 7, *Tō-Asia*, Part III, Tokyo 1963, fig. 191.   For one of the earliest specimens in the series, dated 251 A.D., see *Sekai Kokōgaku Taikei, op cit.*, p. 79, fig. 229.

44 JAR
Six Dynasties
4th to 5th century A.D.
Stoneware, Yüeh-yao
Diam. 5 ³/₄ in.   *C-148*

Four square handles are set in axial position on the shoulder of this globular jar which has a short neck and a slightly concave base. The decoration proper is restricted to two series of finely incised grooves, one located just below the base of the neck and the other lower on the body. The grey porcelaneous stoneware is covered with a greyish-green glaze that stops short of the foot. Four large iron-brown spots are disposed symmetrically between the handles, and a series of smaller ones adorn the mouth rim.

45 *STANDING ATTENDANT*

Northern Wei
First part of 6th century A.D.
Painted pottery
H. 7 1/4 in.   *C-156*

This tomb figurine is said to have been part of a set excavated in the fall of 1948 near the village of Chun-tao ts'un, Lo-yang fu in Honan province.   The large-headed attendant wears a crested hat and a long, wide-sleeved coat over baggy trousers. [1]   The right side of the body is perforated with a fairly large, slanting hole just above the elbow.   There is another hole inside the right hand.   Both holes were made to insert an object or a weapon.   Traces of white slip and pigments are visible over the grey pottery.

(1)   See Jean-Pierre Dubosc, *Exhibition of Chinese Art*, Venice 1954, p. 96, fig. 304 for the same type of headgear and garments.

46 *STANDING OFFICIAL*

Six Dynasties
6th century A.D.
Painted pottery
H. 23 in.   *C-144*

Unlike many examples of this distinctive series of officials, this funerary statuette does not have obviously un-Chinese facial features, even though the person it portrays might still be of Mongol or Turkish stock.   The crescent-shaped eyes are almost completely closed, a rather unusual characteristic.   The long robe of Chinese style with wide flaring sleeves is partly covered by a leather waistcoat strapped at the shoulders. [1]   The dark grey ware still bears traces of pigments.

(1) For similar garments, see René-Yvon Lefebvre d'Argencé, *Chinese Ceramics in the Avery Brundage Collection*, San Francisco 1967, Pl. XVII-A; and Ezekiel Schloss, *Foreigners in Ancient Chinese Art*, New York 1969, fig. 53.

47 CAMEL

Northern Wei
First part of 6th century A.D.
Painted pottery
H. 10 ¹/₂ in.   *C-113*

This funerary figurine of a camel is standing squarely on a thin slab.   The small head is raised.   The packsaddle consists of a blanket which fits around the humps. Two large wicker baskets are tied up with a rope or a leather strap and rest on the blanket on either side of the animal.   With the exception of the legs, the camel is covered with a thick wooly fur which has grown into a mane on the top of the head and the nape of the neck. [1]   With the exception of the mane, the camel is painted red; the packsaddle and baskets are black.

(1)   Compare René-Yvon Lefebvre d'Argencé, *Chinese Ceramics in the Avery Brundage Collection,* San Francisco 1967, Pl. XVI-A; and Osaka Museum and Center of Asian Art and Culture, *Osaka Exchange Exhibition, Paintings from the Abe Collection and Other Masterpieces of Chinese Art*, Osaka and San Francisco 1970, p. 137, fig. 89.

48 INK-STONE

Six Dynasties
5th to 6th century A.D.
Sandstone
H. 5 in. Diam. 5 1/2 in. C-137

Shaped like a millstone, this object consists of two slabs. The lower one rests on three diminutive bears and has a slightly recessed rim to make room for the close-fitting lip of the upper slab which serves as a lid. The dome-shaped surface of this upper slab is covered with an irregular network of small incised lozenges and topped by a winged chimera.[1] Planted firmly on its four legs, this fabulous feline is a miniature of the "life-size" or gigantic statues which guarded the tombs of the period.[2] The underside of the lower slab is carved with the large chevron motives that radiate from the center.

(1) A lamp stand in the same material, technique and general style has been excavated in Shansi province and ascribed to the "Northern Dynasties" (4th to 6th centuries A.D.). It is illustrated in *Ch'üan-kuo Chi-pen Chien-she Kung-ch'eng Chung Ch'u-t'u Wen-wu Chan-lan T'u-lu*, Shanghai 1955, Pl. 37.

(2) Compare Alexander Soper, "Chinese Sculpture [in the Avery Brundage Collection]," *Apollo*, Vol. LXXXIV, No. 54, August 1966, p. 108, fig. 7.

49 EWER

Late Six Dynasties or T'ang
6th to 9th century A.D.
Steatite
H. 3 3/4 in. C-111

Turned on the wheel and then carefully polished, this ewer illustrates an unusual and not altogether harmonious blending of ceramic and metallic traditions. The ovoid body rests on a flat base. The handle, which consists of an oversized thumb-piece placed on top of a small faceted loop, is set at a right angle to the spout. The latter is in the shape of a neckless feline head.[1]

(1) To our knowledge, the only similar item that has been published is to be found in *Catalogue of the Archaeological Collection in the Museum of the Faculty of Letters, Kyoto University*, Part 3, Kyoto 1963, p. 145, fig. 193.

50 AMPHORA

Sui or Early T'ang
6th to 7th century A.D.
Glazed stoneware
H. 13 1/4 in. C-133

This funerary amphora has a bulging ovoid body, a small flat base, and a slender spool-like neck ending in a cup-shaped mouth with an everted rim. Two large, two-stranded, bow-shaped handles terminate in crested dragon heads that bite the rim of the vessel. The lower lips of the dragons are inordinately long and hang down below the mouth line. The three studs that are applied on each of the handles may be "fossilized" vertebrae. The finely crazed neutral glaze which has flaked in parts was applied over the upper part of the vessel. The lower part reveals a hard greyish-white body. [1]

(1) Compare *Sekai Tōji Zenshū*, Vol. 9, Tokyo 1956, p. 167, fig. 16; and Ireneus László Legeza, *A Descriptive and Illustrated Catalogue of the Malcolm MacDonald Collection of Chinese Ceramics*, London 1972, Pl. IV, no. 9.

51   *TWO LADIES*

Sui or Early T'ang
Late 6th to early 7th century A.D.
Glazed pottery
H. 7 ³/₈ in.   C-1066 and 1067

These two slender and elegant figurines represent young ladies from Kucha, one of the four oasis garrisons that the T'ang Empire maintained in Central Asia. They sport an elaborate, crested coiffure and wear long-sleeved, conical robes. One is a dancer, the other holds a pitcher.[1]   The buff clay is covered with a creamy glaze that has flanked in parts.

(1)   For a set of comparable figurines, see Ezekiel Schloss, *Foreigners in Ancient Chinese Art*, New York 1969, Pl. 29.

52 *WARRIOR*
Sui or Early T'ang
Late 6th to early 7th century A.D.
Glazed pottery
H. 19 in.   *C-136*

Standing rigidly at attention, this warrior (probably a lancer even though his hands are not pierced), whose facial features denote his Khotanese origin,[1] wears an armor over a short blouse and a skirt with long foliated tails. The plain undergarment reaches down to the ankles. The elaborate helmet and armor were probably fashioned from a relatively supple material such as leather; they are elaborately cut out into stylized floral patterns. The hard-fired pinkish clay is coated with straw-colored glaze applied over a white slip and showing an intricate network of fine crackles.[2]

(1) Compare Jane Gaston Mahler, *The Westerners among the Figurines of the T'ang Dynasty of China*, Rome 1959, Pls. XXVII and XXVIII-a.
(2) See Alfred Salmony, *Sammlung J. F. H. Menten, Chinesische Grabfunde und Bronzen*, Zurich 1948, fig. 68 for an almost identical figurine.

53 *FEMALE MUSICIAN*

Mid-T'ang
First part of 8th century A.D.
Painted pottery
H. 6 ³/₄ in.   *C-121*

This graceful castanet player was originally part of a group of funerary figurines representing musicians and possibly dancers.   She wears a high, elaborate coiffure and a long flowing robe, the lower part of which is spread out in front of her.[1] Traces of a white slip and polychrome pigments are still visible over the brownish clay.

(1) Jacques P. van Goidsenhoven illustrates a similar figurine as part of a set of five musicians and dancers in *La Céramique Chinoise*, Brussels 1954, Pl. XIX.

54 *STANDING LADY*

Mid T'ang
First part of 8th century A.D.
Painted pottery
H. 14 ³/₄ in.   *C-114*

This plump, dignified lady belongs to a large group of funerary figurines that exemplify one type of feminine beauty much appreciated at the court during the early decades of the 8th century.[1]   Most of the statuette is covered by a rather thick layer of dry mud, but where exposed the red clay retains in parts traces of a white slip and of multicolor pigments.

(1) For similar figurines, see for instance: Mario Prodan, *The Art of the T'ang Potter*, New York 1961, fig. 34; *Sekai Tōji Zenshū*, Vol. 9, Tokyo 1956, figs. 142 and 143; and Ch'in T'ing-yü, *Chung-kuo Ku-tai T'ao-su I-shu*, Shanghai 1955, Pl. 45.

55 *SEATED LION*

T'ang
Ca. 8th century A.D.
Painted pottery
H. 6 in.　　　　*C-153*

The tall, powerfully built animal is seated on a rectangular base. It growls and claws the air with its left paw in a menacing gesture. Each component of the head and body is clearly delineated. The hood-like curly mane falls on the shoulder and back, and the open mouth reveals fangs and teeth.[1] Despite its small dimensions, this statuette exudes brutal force and vitality. Traces of white slip and polychrome pigments are still perceptible on various parts of the head and body. The base is perforated, and the inside is hollow.

(1)　See No. 34 in this catalogue for a gilt bronze lion of similar posture.

56 JAR

T'ang
Late 7th to 8th century A.D.
Glazed pottery
H. 10 ¹/₂ in.   *C-132*

This jar has an ovoid body with a short cylindrical neck, a thick everted lip, a slightly splayed foot and a relatively small and flat base.   The buff ware is covered with amber-brown glaze.   The glaze has been allowed to run freely and, for the most part, stops short of the foot.

57   LIEN

T'ang
Late 7th to 8th century A.D.
Glazed pottery
H. 4 5/8 in.   *C-122*

Remotely derived from Warring States and Han bronze prototypes,[1] this cylindrical vessel[2] stands on three small baluster feet.   The sides are ornamented with a series of seventeen grooves.   The buff-white ware is covered with a leaf-green glaze on the outside and a yellow glaze on the inside.   The base and the underside of the feet are unglazed.[3]

(1)   See for instance No. 10 in this catalogue.
(2)   Published: *Sekai Tōji Zenshū*, Vol. 9, Tokyo 1956, Pl. 91 where dated 680–750 A.D.
(3)   For comparable examples see Robert L. Hobson, *The Eumorfopoulos Catalogue*, Vol. I, London 1926, Pl. LVIII, 373, and John Ayers, *The Baur Collection, Chinese Ceramics*, Vol. I, Geneva 1968, A3, No. 118.

.

58 *JAR*

T'ang
Late 7th to 8th century A.D.
Glazed pottery
H. 7 in.   *C-1063*

Standing on a flat base, this rare jar has a wide ovoid body, a short concave neck and an everted mouth rim.   The white clay is covered with a deep blue glaze that stops short of the foot.   Two fine incised lines run around the shoulder.[1]

(1) For comparable examples see Jean-Pierre Dubosc, *Exhibition of Chinese Art*, Venice 1954, fig. 332; and Michael Sullivan, *Chinese Ceramics, Bronzes and Jades in the Collection of Sir Alan and Lady Barlow*, London 1963, C.253.

59 CUP

T'ang
Late 7th to 8th century A.D.
Glazed pottery
H. 2 1/4 in.   *C-126*

This bell-shaped cup stands on a fairly high, splayed foot and has a relatively large ring handle.   A circular ridge placed on the lower part of the body echoes the overhanging lip.   The buff clay is covered on both the inside and the outside with a faintly iridescent blue glaze.[1]   On the outside, the glaze stops shortly below the ridge mentioned above.

(1)   For a similar piece, see *Sekai Tōji Zenshū*, Vol. 9, Tokyo 1956, Pl. 72; and Mizuno Seiichi, *Tōki Zenshū*, No. 25, *Tō San-sai*, Tokyo 1965, Pl. 45-b.

60 BOX WITH COVER

T'ang
Late 7th to 8th century A.D.
Glazed pottery
H. 1 1/4 in.   *C-108*

The box and its cover form a shallow cylinder with flat top and bottom.   The top of the lid is slightly recessed and so is the base, but otherwise the surface of the box bears no ornamentation.   The buff ware is covered with a dark blue glaze on the outside and a yellow glaze on the inside of the box proper.   An ochre slip has been applied on the inside of the lid.

(1)   Compare *Sekai Tōji Zenshū*, Vol. 9, Tokyo 1956, Pl. 72.

61 *EWER*

T'ang
Late 7th to 8th century A.D.
Glazed stoneware
H. 8 in.   *C-102*

The pear-shaped body ends in a constricted foot with a flat base.   The fairly high neck leads to a flaring mouth with an overhanging lip.   Opposite the conical "threaded" spout, which has been restored, there is a large double-stranded handle. Two smaller handles of the same type are set in axial position.   The buff clay has burnt red on the unglazed base and foot.   Everywhere else it is covered by a white slip and an olive-yellow glaze.   Beneath the glaze a pattern of punch marks covers the entire body in twenty-four successive lines. [1]

(1)   This decor may be unusual but the shape and glaze are well attested; see for instance Hsien-ch'i Tseng and Robert Paul Dart, *The Charles B. Hoyt Collection*, Vol. 1, Boston 1964, Pl. 82.

62   THREE-LEGGED JAR

T'ang
Late 7th to 8th century A.D.
Pottery with three-colored glazes
H. 6 1/4 in.   *C-142*

The wide globular body is supported by three feline, paw-like legs.   The short, slightly concave neck ends in a widely flaring mouth rim.   The shoulder and lower part of the jar are slightly recessed with the effect that the median part of the jar is encircled by a wide band in relief.   The white clay is covered with mottled amber, green and white glazes.   The glazes form an irregular pattern of petals on the shoulder and stop short of the bottom while covering part of the legs. [1]

(1)   For a similar piece, see Mizuno Seiichi, *Tōki Zenshū*, No. 25, *Tō San-sai*, Tokyo 1965, Pl. 24.

63   *TRAY*

T'ang
Late 7th to 8th century A.D.
Pottery with three-colored glazes
Diam. 6 $^{15}/_{16}$ in.   *C-1065*

Standing on three small splayed feet, the dish has low, rounded sides and an everted rim.   An incised floral medallion occupies the center of the dish.   This medallion is surrounded by six incised, fungi-form clouds.   The medallion is colored with blue, amber and green glazes and the clouds with blue and amber glazes.[1]   With the exception of the base and underside of the feet where the pinkish clay is exposed, the dish is covered with a neutral glaze applied over a white slip.   All these glazes are slightly iridescent.

(1)   For a similar tray see *Sekai Tōji Zenshū*, Vol. 9, Tokyo 1956, fig. 97.

64 JAR WITH LID

T'ang
Late 7th to 8th century A.D.
Pottery with three-colored glazes
H. 2 7/8 in.   *C-110*

This small jar has a globular and neckless body resting on a flat base. The flat, two-stepped lid is surmounted by a bud-like knob. The buff ware is covered on the outside with streaked cream, brown and green glazes. The base is entirely glazed with the exception of two spur marks.[1]

(1) For a similar piece, see Robert Treat Paine, Jr., *The Charles B. Hoyt Collection Memorial Exhibition February 13-March 30, 1952*, Boston 1952, fig. 107.

65 SMALL JAR

T'ang
Late 7th to 8th century A.D.
Pottery with three-colored glazes
H. 2 3/8 in.   *C-127*

This small jar has a wide globular body with a gently sloping shoulder and a rounded base. The light buff ware is covered on the outside with blue, white and yellow glazes. The white and yellow glazes form seven large leaf-like spots around the shoulder; the blue glaze stops short of the base.

66 SMALL JAR

T'ang
Late 7th to 8th century A.D.
Pottery with three-colored glazes
H. 2 1/2 in.   *C-123*

This small jar has a globular body, a sturdy circular foot and a wide mouth with everted lip. With the exception of the foot and base, the outside of the jar and the inside of the mouth rim are covered with white and light green streaked glazes over a white slip. Owing to prolonged burial, the green glaze has become partly iridescent. The inside of the jar below the lip is covered with a yellow glaze.

67 HUMPED OX

T'ang
Late 7th to 8th century A.D.
Glazed pottery
H. 5 1/4 in.   L. 6 1/2 in.   *C-128*

This funerary figurine of an ox has the appearance and slightly humoristic touch of a child's toy.   Tensely drawn over the head and sides, its skin is all wrinkled and flaccid in the area of the neck and legs.[1]   The animal stands on a small rectangular slab.   The white clay is covered with a light amber glaze, except for the head where the glaze is almost white.   The body is hollow.

(1)   There is a very similar piece in the Avery Brundage Collection (B72 P14).

68   *HORSE AND RIDER*

T'ang
Late 7th to 8th century A.D.
Glazed pottery
H. 16 in.   L. 13 ¹/₂ in.   C-152

This funerary figurine of a woman riding a Bactrian horse is supported by a small thin slab.   The horse is covered with a cream and brown glaze which is slightly iridescent as a result of intensive degradation.   The rider wears a gown with a thick green and brown glaze.   Her hair is done in a high chignon, and her unglazed face retains traces of a white slip.   Wherever exposed, the clay is light grey.

69 EWER

T'ang
618 to 906 A.D.
Porcelaneous ware
H. 6 1/2 in.   C-140

The silhouette of this ewer is rather unusual as the near spherical body is surmounted by a widely flaring trumpet-like neck which is linked to the shoulder by a loop handle.   A small conical spout is set high on the shoulder on the side opposite the handle.   The buff body, exposed at the base, is covered with a finely crazed neutral glaze applied over a white slip. [1]

(1)   See Robert L. Hobson, *The Eumorfopoulos Collection*, Vol. 1, London 1926, Pl. LXXI, 500 for a comparable piece.

70 JAR

T'ang
618 to 906 A.D.
Porcelaneous ware
H. 4 3/8 in.   C-106

This jar has a wide ovoid body with a flat base and a short concave neck ending in a slightly flaring lip.   The hard-fired buff clay is covered with a finely crazed neutral glaze applied over a white slip.   The base is unglazed. [1]

(1)   For comparable pieces, see *Sekai Tōji Zenshū*, Vol. 9, Tokyo 1956, Pl. 28; and Kobayashi Taichirō, *Tōki Zenshū*, No. 12, *Tō Sō no Hakuji*, Pls. 18 and 19.

71   *EWER*

T'ang
618 to 906 A.D.
Porcelain, Hsing-yao type
H. 7 1/2 in.   *C-141*

The ovoid body of this ewer rests on a shallow, slightly flaring foot and a flat base.[1]   The short, slightly conical spout, placed high on the shoulder, is surmounted by an applied animal mask (possibly a wolf) in high relief.   On the opposite side, a handle shaped like a lion spans the entire length of the high neck. The arched lion stands on the shoulder and grasps the mouth rim with its mouth and forepaws.   The light grey body is exposed on the foot and base, but the rest of the vessel is covered with a white glaze.[2]   The inside of the ewer is also glazed.

(1)   Published: Mario Prodan, *The Art of the T'ang Potter*, New York 1961, Pl. 105.
(2)   See also No. 72 in this catalogue.

72   *EWER*

T'ang
618 to 906 A.D.
Porcelain, Hsing-yao type
H. 3 1/3 in.   *C-146*

This miniature ewer belongs to the same category as no. C-141 above.   It is, however, less refined.   Its lion handle, for example, does not have the sharp definition nor the vitality of that of C-141.   The short conical spout is frilled at the base instead of being surmounted by an animal mask.[1]

(1)   See Robert L. Hobson, *The Eumorfopoulos Collection*, Vol. 1, London 1915, Pl. LXXIV, 503. See also Gustaf Lindberg, "Hsing-yao and Ting-yao," *BMFEA*, No. 25, Stockholm 1953, Pl. 38, fig. 32-a and Pl. 39, fig. 32-b; and Bo Gyllensvärd, *Chinese Gold, Silver and Porcelain, The Kempe Collection*, New York 1971, p. 89, fig. 72.

73 DISH

T'ang
618 to 906 A.D.
Porcelain, Hsing-yao type
W. 4 ³/₄ in.   *C-155*

This dish is divided into three leaf-like pointed lobes. The round bottom is
slightly convex. The white glaze shows minute air bubbles and has a bluish
tinge where it has accumulated. It covers all but the foot rim and the recessed
base where the buff body is exposed.[1]   The foot is gritty.

(1) For comparable pieces, see Gustaf Lindberg, "Hsing-yao and Ting-yao," *BMFEA*, No.
25, Stockholm 1953, Pl. 34, fig. 28; Jean-Pierre Dubosc, *Exhibition of Chinese Art*, Venice
1954, fig. 352; Hin-Cheung Lovell, *Illustrated Catalogue of Ting Yao and Related White
Wares in the Percival David Foundation of Chinese Art*, London 1964, Pl. X, fig. 173; and
Bo Gyllensvärd, *Chinese Gold, Silver and Porcelain*, *The Kempe Collection*, New York
1971, fig. 102.

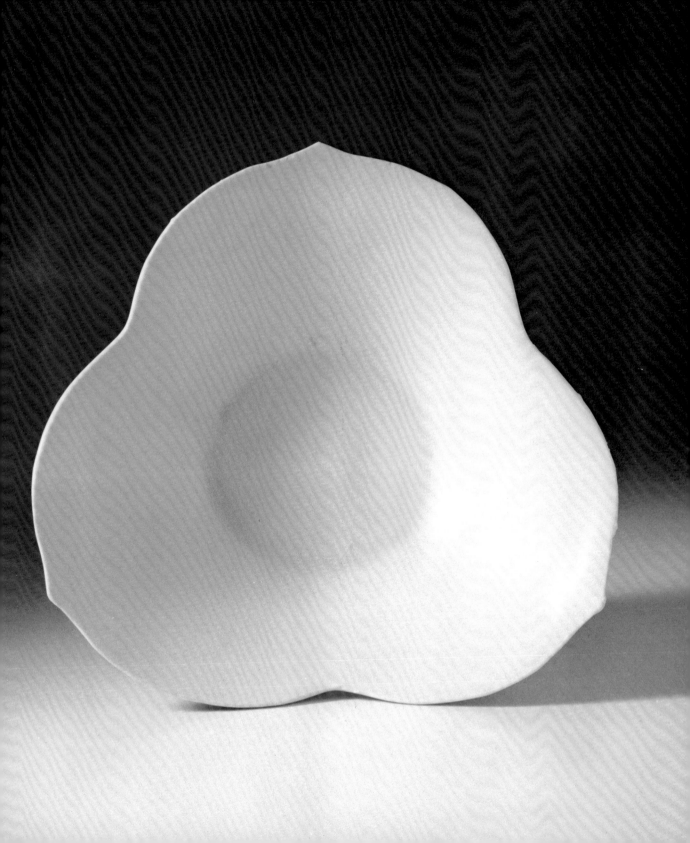

74   SMALL JAR
T'ang
618–906 A.D.
Porcelain, Hsing-yao type
H. 2 1/2 in.   *C-109*

The surface of this very finely potted little jar of globular shape is plain with the exception of two concentric grooves around the mouth.   The slightly pinkish body is covered with a white, uncrazed glaze with a greenish-brown tinge where it has run thick. [1]   The finely carved foot is gritty in parts.

(1)   Compare with Gustaf Lindberg, "Hsing-yao and Ting-yao," *BMFEA*, No. 25, Stockholm 1953, Pl. 54, fig. 50.

75   WATERPOT
T'ang
618 to 906 A.D.
Porcelain, Hsing-yao type
H. 2 in.   *C-1032*

The quadrilobed, globular body rests on three slightly misshapen feet.   There is no neck, but only a wide circular mouth and an everted lip.   The base is unglazed and reveals a white body.   The rest of the vessel is covered with a cream-white glaze with a greenish-brown tinge where it has run thick. [1]

(1)   Jean-Pierre Dubosc in his catalogue, *Exhibition of Chinese Art*, Venice 1954, fig. 359, illustrates a similar piece which is ascribed to the T'ang dynasty and labeled "Possibly Hsing Ware". See also Gustaf Lindberg, "Hsing-yao and Ting-yao," *BMFEA*, No. 25, Stockholm 1953, Pl. 16, fig. 12; and Roger Goepper et al., *Form und Farbe*, Tokyo 1972, fig. 56.

76 *PILGRIM BOTTLE*

Liao
907 to 1126 A.D.
Glazed pottery
H. 11 ¹/₂ in.   *C-143*

The pear-shaped, rather crudely potted body rests on a short, but thick circular foot with a recessed base. The almost vertical, cylindrical spout is off-center. The small, freesculpted loop handle is ornamented with a series of pinched marks which are sometimes compared to a cock's comb.[1]   The upper part of the buff ware is covered with a light amber glaze applied over a white slip.

(1) See for instance Kuroda Genji and Sugimura Yūzō, *Tōki Zenshū*, No. 14, *Ryō no Tōji*, Tokyo 1958, Pl. 20.

77 *SADDLE-GOURD*

Liao
907 to 1126 A.D.
Glazed pottery
H. 11 ¹/₂ in.   *C-135*

This is an imitation in pottery of a leather flask.   It rests on a small oval and slightly concave base.   The narrow, cylindrical spout is placed on one side at the top of the vessel.   Behind it a high ridge, with a central deep notch to insure a better grip, is perforated with two suspension holes.   Both sides are freely incised with leaf scrolls.   The pinkish-brown ware is covered with an iridescent green glaze that stops short of the base. [1]

(1)   Comparable pieces illustrated in Kuroda Genji and Sugimura Yūzō, *Tōki Zenshū*, No. 14, *Ryō no Tōji*, Tokyo 1958, Pls. 4–6.

78 *EWER*

Liao
907 to 1126 A.D.
Glazed pottery
H. 4 in.   C-147

The six-lobed, melon-shaped body rests on a short, but thick circular foot with a recessed base.   The small spout and three-stranded handle are set in axial position.   The small mouth occupies the center of a depressed collar.   Each lobe is decorated with a series of combed semicircles.   With the exception of the base, which reveals a buff ware, the entire piece is covered with thick green glaze.

79 *BOTTLE*

Liao
907 to 1126 A.D.
Glazed pottery
H. 9 1/2 in.   C-130

The pear-shaped body rests on a short but thick circular foot with a recessed base and terminates in a long, slender cylindrical neck with a slightly flaring mouth and an everted lip.   The bases of the neck and shoulder are marked by a couple of incised lines which frame two applied animal masks.   The masks hold large rings in their mouths.   Obviously, all these motifs are reminiscent of bronze prototypes.   With the exception of the recessed base, the reddish-brown ware is covered with a black slip over which a green glaze covers neck, shoulder and foot. The same glaze was used in painting the bold, free-hand floral design that decorates the central zone.[1]   In several parts of the neck and shoulder the glaze has heavily crackled or even flaked away, thus producing a curious snakeskin effect.

(1) In his catalogue, *The George Eumorfopoulos Collection*, Vol. II, London 1926, Pl. LXXIV, B 304, R. L. Hobson attributes a bottle of a similar type and technique to the Sung dynasty and suggests a Honan provenance for it.

80 *CEREMONIAL VASE*

Five Dynasties or Early Sung
10th century A.D.
Porcelaneous stoneware, Celadon
H. 15 ³/₄ in.   *C-1054*

This example of the so-called " 'grey ware' of Yüeh type"[1] has an oviform body that rests on a short and sturdy cylindrical foot. The elongated, ribbed neck opens up in a widely flaring mouth with a rising lip. Two small, two-stranded loop handles have been applied on the base of the neck.[2] The shoulder is delineated by a wavy "piecrust" band and is adorned with a boneless and clawless dragon that rests its head on one of the loop handles. This dragon sports two pairs of antlers, and its entire body is punched with little depressions suggesting scales. The unglazed base reveals the clay which was burnt to a reddish-brown during firing. Otherwise, both the outside and inside are covered with a pale greenish glaze.

(1) See G. St. G. M. Gompertz, *Chinese Celadon Wares*, London 1958, Pls. 19 and ff.
(2) See René-Yvon Lefebvre d'Argencé, *Chinese Ceramics in the Avery Brundage Collection*, San Francisco 1967, p. 68.

81 *FIVE-SPOUTED JAR*

Five Dynasties or Early Sung
10th century A.D.
Porcelaneous stoneware, Li-shui type
H. 10 ³/₄ in.   *C-1000*

The ovoid body of this jar rests on a short, sturdy foot with a recessed base and is stepped in five horizontal lobes.   The neck is cylindrical, and the domed cover is surmounted by a jar-shaped finial.   Five vertical false spouts are located high on the shoulder.   With the exception of the base which reveals the grey clay, the entire surface of the vessel is covered with a highly vitrified and heavily crazed olive-green glaze of the *Li-shui* type. [1]   The inside of the jar is also glazed.

(1)   For comparable pieces see Tokyo National Museum, *Illustrated Catalogue of Old Oriental Ceramics Donated by Mr. Yokogawa*, Tokyo 1953, fig. 101 (labeled Nan Sung Kuan-yao); and Jan Wirgin, "Sung Ceramic Designs," *BMFEA*, No. 42, Stockholm 1970, Pl. 37, fig. a.

82 *JAR WITH COVER*

Northern Sung
10th to 11th century A.D.
Porcelaneous stoneware, Celadon
H. 9 ¹/₂ in.   *C-1053*

The ovoid body rests on a sturdy, slightly splayed foot. The wide, high and cylindrical neck ends in an everted lip. The rim of the domed cover projects beyond the lip, and the knob is in the shape of a bud. A series of double lines is incised at more or less regular intervals over the neck and body. With the exception of the base and rims of the mouth and cover, the entire surface of the jar is covered with a bluish-green glaze that is degraded in parts. Wherever exposed, the clay is either buff or reddish as a result of burning during firing. Such vessels were probably made in Chekiang.

83 *BOWL*

Sung
11th to 12th century A.D.
Porcelaneous stoneware, Northern Celadon
H. 2 ¹/₄ in.   *C-1003*

The bowl rests on a high circular foot and has an everted mouth rim.   The surface is plain with the exception of six low vertical ribs which divide the inside into as many sections.   With the exception of the foot, the entire bowl is covered with an olive-green glaze. [1]

(1)   See Robert L. Hobson, *The Eumorfopoulos Collection*, Vol. II, London 1926, Pl. L, B 187.

84 *BOWL*

Sung
11th to 12th century A.D.
Porcelaneous stoneware, Northern Celadon
H. 2 ¹/₂ in.   *C-1029*

The bowl stands on a fairly high and sturdy foot and has an everted rim.   The inside is divided into six vertical sections by low ribs.   The lower part of the outside is decorated with a wide band of deeply carved leaves.   The foot rim is unglazed and burnt reddish-brown.   The rest of the bowl, including the base, is covered with an olive-green glaze.   A small and slightly misshapen circle is incised on the base.

85 *BOWL*

Sung
11th to 12th century A.D.
Porcelaneous stoneware, Northern Celadon
Diam. 8 in.   *C-1002*

The inside of the bowl is divided into six sections by six ridges.   The carved design consists of a large central flower, probably a peony, and of leaves and petals on the periphery. [1]   An olive-green glaze covers the entire surface of the bowl with the exception of the foot rim.

(1)   See *Sekai Tōji Zenshū*, Vol. 10, Tokyo 1955, Pl. 32 for a similar design; Michael Sullivan, *Chinese Ceramics, Bronzes and Jades in the Collection of Sir Alan and Lady Barlow*, London 1963, Pl. 65-a; and Koyama Fujio, *Chūgoku Tōji, Jō*, Vol. 2 in the series *Idemitsu Bijutsukan Sensho*, Tokyo 1970, Pl. 27.

86 BOWL

Sung
11th to 12th century A.D.
Porcelaneous stoneware, Northern Celadon
Diam. 5 ³/₈ in.   *C-1049*

The conical bowl with slightly rounded sides and an everted mouth rim stands on a small circular foot.   The inside is decorated with a carved lily-scroll surrounded by combed wavy lines.   The foot rim and the convex base are unglazed and burnt reddish-brown, otherwise the rest of the vessel is covered with a faintly crazed olive-green glaze. [1]

(1) Robert L. Hobson, *The Eumorfopoulos Collection*, Vol. II, London 1926, Pl. LIV, B 192. See also Jean-Pierre Dubosc, *Exhibition of Chinese Art*, Venice 1954, fig. 410; Michael Sullivan, *Chinese Ceramics, Bronzes and Jades in the Collection of Sir Alan and Lady Barlow*, London 1963, Pl. 66-a; and Ireneus László Legeza, *A Descriptive and Illustrated Catalogue of the Malcolm MacDonald Collection of Chinese Ceramics*, London 1972, Pl. XXI, No. 66.

87 JAR
Sung
11th to 12th century A.D.
Porcelaneous stoneware, Northern Celadon
H. 6 ³/₄ in.   *C-1001*

The ovoid body rests on a short and sturdy foot.[1]   The vertical, cylindrical neck
ends in an everted mouth rim.   The shoulder and lower part of the body are
decorated with narrow bands of carved overlapping petals while the carved
decoration of the central zone consists of a scroll of peonies with combed shading.
With the exception of the foot rim and part of the bottom, the entire jar is covered
with an olive-green glaze.

(1) Published: Robert L. Hobson, *The Eumorfopoulos Collection*, Vol. II, London 1926, Pl.
L, B 189.

88 CEREMONIAL JAR

Late Northern Sung
Ca. 11th century
Porcelaneous stoneware, Lung-ch'üan Celadon
H. 10 ¹/₂ in.   *C-1044*

The body of this jar consists of a short and narrow cylindrical neck, a three-stepped pyramidal shoulder and a barrel-shaped belly.   A four-clawed dragon, modeled in high relief, winds around the neck and shoulder.   On the belly is carved a row of tall lotus petals.   The dome-shaped lid is surmounted by a bird in the round. With the exception of the mouth and foot rim and the inner rim of the cover, the entire jar is covered with a clear bluish-green glaze.   The exposed rims reveal a buff-grey body.

(1)   Compare with Seizo Hayashiya and Gakuji Hasebe, *Chinese Ceramics*, Tokyo 1966, fig. 130; and Tokyo National Museum, *Illustrated Catalogue of Old Oriental Ceramics Donated by Mr. Yokogawa*, Tokyo 1953, fig. 99. The same piece is also illustrated and ascribed to the Northern Sung in *Sekai Tōji Zenshū*, Vol. 10, Tokyo 1955, fig. 32.

89 WINE JAR WITH LID

Sung
12th to 13th century
Porcelaneous stoneware, Lung-ch'üan Celadon
W. 4 in.   *C-1059*

The globular body stands on a slightly concave base. A small, but sturdy spout juts out from the shoulder. The neck is short and has vertical sides. The bulging part of the body is ribbed, and the top of the flat lid is decorated with a partly carved, partly incised five-petaled flower. The grey body is exposed at the base, the mouth rim and the inside of the cover. The rest of the jar is entirely covered with an even, unctuous, light green glaze.

90 INCENSE BURNER

Southern Sung
12th to 13th century A.D.
Porcelaneous stoneware, Lung-ch'üan Celadon
H. 2 7/8 in.   *C-1058*

Derived from a bronze *li*, this incense burner stands on three slightly splayed legs. It has a depressed globular bowl, a short cylindrical neck and an everted, flattened mouth rim. Shallow flanges run up the legs and the side of the bowl. The grey ware is exposed at the tips of the legs where it was largely burnt brown during firing. The rest of the vessel is covered with an unctuous grey-green glaze of *Kinuta* type.[1]

(1) There are numerous examples of this type of incense burner. See for instance Robert L. Hobson, *The Eumorfopoulos Collection*, Volume II, London 1927, Pl. XXIX, B 106, and Pl. XXX, B 107 and B 108; and Ch'en Wan-li, *Chung-kuo Ch'ing Tz'u Shih-lüeh*, Hong Kong 1972, Pl. 16.

91 *DISH*

Southern Sung
12th to 13th century A.D.
Porcelain, Hsiu-nei ssu or Lung-ch'üan Ta-yao Celadon
Diam. 4 1/2 in.   *C-1060*

This dish with slightly flaring sides and an everted mouth rim stands on a large, shallow foot. With the exception of the foot rim which reveals a white body turned reddish-brown during firing, the entire piece is covered with a thick, even bluish-green glaze.

Much has been written about this enigmatic ware. We retain here Fujio Koyama's and G. St. G. M. Gompertz' attribution which appears to be the most convincing in the present state of knowledge. [1]

(1) See *Sekai Tōji Zenshū*, Vol. 10, Tokyo 1955, Pl. 42; G. St. G. M. Gompertz, *Chinese Celadon Wares*, London 1958, Pl. 61; and Koyama Fujio, *Idemitsu Bijutsukan Sensho*, Vol. 2, *Chūgoku Tōji, Jō*, Tokyo 1970, Pl. 46.

92 *BOWL*

Southern Sung
12th to 13th century A.D.
Porcelaneous stoneware, Lung-ch'üan Celadon
Diam. 6 1/2 in.   *C-1004*

This deep open bowl with rounded sides stands on a small shallow foot and is decorated with a large band of carved lotus petals on the outside. The grey-green glaze which covers the entire piece with the exception of the foot rim is of *Kinuta* type. [1]

(1) This is a very common shape which is represented in a number of collections. See for instance John Ayers, *The Seligman Collection of Oriental Art*, Vol. II, London 1964, Pl. LVII, D 169 and D 177; and Jan Wirgin, "Sung Ceramic Designs," *BMFEA*, No. 42, Stockholm 1970, fig. 42: c: 2.

93 BOX WITH COVER
Five Dynasties or Early Sung
Ca. 10th century A.D.
Porcelaneous white ware
Diam. 4 ⁷/₈ in.   *C-1019*

The lower and upper sections of this cylindrical box are slightly rounded.   With the exception of the recessed base and that part where the inner lips meet, the entire piece, inside and outside, is covered with an ivory glaze.   Where exposed, the white body has turned ochre during firing.[1]

(1)   See Jean-Pierre Dubosc's catalogue, *Exhibition of Chinese Art*, Venice 1954, fig. 552, where a similar box is labeled "Sung dynasty or earlier."

94 JAR
Five Dynasties or Early Sung
Ca. 10th century A.D.
Porcelaneous white ware
H. 3 ³/₄ in.   *C-1042*

The cylindrical body rests on a small circular foot.   The neck is practically vertical and straight.   An ivory glaze of the *Ting* type covers the upper part of the inside and, on the outside, stops short of the foot where the buff body is exposed.

95 SMALL PLATE
Five Dynasties or Early Sung
10th century A.D.
Porcelaneous white ware
Diam. 7 $^1/_8$ in.   *C-112*

This shallow dish has slanting sides and an everted flat rim with a raised border. The foot is very shallow.   With the exception of the outer rim where the buff ware is exposed, an ivory glaze of the *Ting* type covers the entire surface, including the partly gritty base. [1]

(1)   For a similar shape, see Henry Trubner, *Chinese Ceramics from the Prehistoric Period through Ch'ien Lung*, Los Angeles 1952, fig. 97.

96 BOX WITH COVER
Northern Sung
Ca. 10th century A.D.
Porcelaneous white ware
W. 2 ⅝ in.   *C-154*

The center of the lid of this trefoil box is adorned with a floral medallion consisting of seven petals in relief surrounded by a beaded border. Another beaded border underlines the contour of the lid. With the exception of the base and rim and part of the interior of the lid, which reveal a pinkish body, the entire piece is covered with an ivory glaze of the *Ting* type, with a greenish-brown tinge where it has run thick. [1]

(1) For a comparable piece, see Michael Sullivan, *Chinese Ceramics, Bronzes and Jades in the Collection of Sir Alan and Lady Barlow*, London 1953, Pl. 27.

97 BOX WITH COVER
Northern Sung
Ca. 10th century A.D.
Porcelaneous white ware
W. 3 ⅝ in.   *C-1061*

This unusual, butterfly-shaped box was probably made in imitation of a metallic prototype. [1] On the cover a molded design of two confronted ducks perched upon the loose ends of an elaborately knotted ribbon stands in low relief against a background of small circles that simulate ring matting. [2] In all likelihood, this motif symbolizes happiness in wedlock. [3] Except for the rims, which reveal a white porcelaneous body, the entire piece is covered with a mottled ivory glaze of the *Ting* type. There are three spur marks on the base.

(1) A butterfly-shaped silver box with comparable design was found in the tomb of Wang Chien who died in 918 A.D. See *The Royal Tomb of Wang Chien of the Former Shu*, Peking 1964, p. 33 and Pl. XXXVII, figs. 1–3.
(2) See for instance Bo Gyllensvärd, *Chinese Gold and Silver in the Carl Kempe Collection*, Stockholm 1953, fig. 139.
(3) For variants of this motif, see for instance Bo Gyllensvärd, *op. cit.*, same plate, and *Chinese Ceramics in the Carl Kempe Collection*, Stockholm 1964, p. 147, fig. 458.

98 *EWER*

Sung
11th to 12th century A.D.
Porcelain, Ting ware
H. 6 1/2 in.   C-1017

The globular body with a marked shoulder line ends in a tall, cylindrical neck that widens toward the mouth. The two-stranded handle makes a right angle just before reaching the neck. The spout is coarsely modeled and slightly off-center. The base of the neck is enclosed in a low-relief ring, and the shoulder is incised with a continuous design of overlapping palmettes. The lower part of the body is adorned with a wide band of partly incised, partly covered overlapping petals. The white ware, including part of the base and the sturdy foot, is covered with a white glaze with a slight ivory tint.[1]

(1) Compare Jan Wirgin, "Sung Ceramic Designs," *BMFEA,* No. 42, Stockholm 1942, Pl. 57, i.

99   *SMALL DISH*

Sung
11th to 12th century A.D.
Porcelain, Ting ware
Diam. 5 ³/₈ in.   *C-1018*

This small dish has slightly rounded, conical sides and rests on a small circular foot. The interior is incised with elongated S-shaped, double-line petals that radiate from the center and seem to revolve counterclockwise. With the exception of the copper-bound mouth rim, the entire bowl is covered with a white, ivory-tinted glaze.[1]

(1)   Compare with Hin-cheung Lovell, *Illustrated Catalogue of Ting Yao and Related White Wares in the Percival David Foundation of Chinese Art*, London 1964, fig. 113; and Ireneus László Legeza, *A Descriptive and Illustrated Catalogue of the Malcolm MacDonald Collection of Chinese Ceramics*, London 1972, Pl. L, No. 150.

100   *DISH*

Sung
11th to 12th century A.D.
Porcelain, Ting ware
Diam. 6 ³/₄ in.   *C-1031*

The center of the inside of the dish is incised with a round panel showing a "dancing" dragon of the *ch'ih* type.[1]   The dragon is so simplified and conventionalized that its spiralling legs and tail are hard to tell from the cloud- or flame-like streamers that are attached to them.   The outside of the rounded sides are incised with three rows of overlapping lotus petals.   With the exception of the mouth and foot rims, the white body of the entire piece is covered with an ivory glaze. The foot is finely carved, although not without some irregularities.

(1)   See Jan Wirgin, "Sung Ceramic Designs," *BMFEA*, No. 42, Stockholm 1970, Pls. 69 and 70.

101 *HARE*
Sung
11th to 12th century A.D.
Porcelain, Ting ware
L. 1 1/16 in.   C-1016

This tiny animal in the round rests on a flat base with irregular contours.   The white ware is covered with the characteristically ivory-tinted white glaze.   *Ting-yao* hares or rabbits are quite rare, even though a variety of Sung kilns did produce a number of small objects representing these animals.[1]

(1)   See for instance Hin-cheung Lovell, *Illustrated Catalogue of Ting Yao and Related White Wares in the Percival David Foundation of Chinese Art*, London 1964, Pl. IV, fig. 124; Kobayashi Taichirō, *Tōki Zenshū*, No. 12, *Tō Sō no Hakuji*, Tokyo 1957, fig. 59 (lower); and Robert Treat Paine, Jr., *The Charles B. Hoyt Collection Memorial Exhibition, February 13-March 30, 1952*, Boston 1952, fig. 300.

102 *BOWL*
Sung
11th to 12th century A.D.
Porcelain, Ting ware
Diam. 8 1/4 in.   C-1051

Very thinly potted, this deep bowl has a rounded, slightly flaring mouth rim and a shallow circular foot.   It is covered with an ivory glaze.[1]   The surface is otherwise quite plain.   Three large concentric circles are incised on the base.

(1)   For comparable examples, see for instance Gustaf Lindberg, "Hsing-yao and Ting-yao," *BMFEA*, No. 25, Stockholm 1953, Pl. 78, fig. 67; and Jan Wirgin, "Sung Ceramic Designs," *BMFEA*, No. 42, Stockholm 1970, Pl. 67-b.

103 TWO BOWLS
Northern Sung
10th to 12th century A.D.
Porcelain, Ch'ing-pai ware
Diam. 4 7/8 in.   C-1026

These two conical bowls, which do not form a pair, are covered with a light blue glaze. The unglazed bases reveal an almost white body that was burnt to a buff color during firing. Variants of sketchy silhouettes of three birds in flight are incised on the inside of each bowl.[1]

(1) Compare with Jan Wirgin, "Sung Ceramic Designs," *BMFEA*, No. 42, Stockholm 1970, Pl. 18-b.

104 DISH
Northern Sung
10th to 12th century A.D.
Porcelain, Ch'ing-pai ware?
Diam. 5 1/2   C-1033

The bottom of this deep dish with a slightly concave base is incised with a large and rather sketchy floral spray. With the exception of the mouth rim which is bound in a copper rim, the entire piece is covered with a faintly bluish glaze that is heavily crazed.

105 EWER
Southern Sung
11th to 12th century A.D.
Porcelain, Ch'ing-pai ware
H. 5 in.   C-1057

Shaped like a double gourd, this ewer has a long, elbowed spout and a handle in the form of an arched *ch'ih* dragon. Except for the gritty base which reveals a buff-white clay, the entire vessel is covered with a light blue glaze that contains innumerable bubbles.[1]

(1) Many such objects have been excavated in the Philippines in recent years. See for instance Leandro and Cecilia Locsin, *Oriental Ceramics Discovered in the Philippines*, Rutland [1967], Pl. 79; and John M. Addis, "Chinese Porcelain Found in the Philippines," *TOCS*, Vol. 37, 1967–1969, London 1970, Pl. 32-b (center).

106 *MEI-P'ING VASE*
Southern Sung
12th to 13th century A.D.
Porcelain, Ch'ing-pai ware
H. 10 in.   *C-1024*

By *Ch'ing-pai* standards the greenish-blue tinted glaze is rather thick.   It covers
the entire vase with the exception of a small irregular band just above the base.[1]
The body is light grey.   The base is recessed.

(1)   For a similar shape and glaze, see Robert L. Hobson, *The Eumorfopoulos Collection*, Vol. II,
London 1927, Pl. XI, B 34.

107 *BOX WITH COVER*
Southern Sung
12th to 13th century A.D.
Porcelain, Ch'ing-pai ware
Diam. 2 ⁵/₈ in.   *C-1046*

The outside of this round box is decorated with molded designs; a floral spray on the slightly domed top of the lid and two rows of overlapping petals on the sides of both the lid and the box itself.[1]   The white body is exposed at the rim of the cover, the base and, rather unexpectedly, the lowest row of petals.   Everywhere else the box is covered with a light blue glaze.

(1) For a similarly decorated piece, see Jan Wirgin, "Sung Ceramic Designs," *BMFEA*, No. 42, Stockholm 1970, Pl. 32-c.

108 *BOWL*
Southern Sung or Yüan
13th to 14th century A.D.
Porcelain, Ch'ing-pai ware
Diam. 7 ¹/₈ in.   *C-1020*

The inside of this bowl with rounded sides is decorated with an elaborate molded design.   The central circular panel contains a pair of phoenixes while the six outer panels frame flower arrangements, all different from one another.   The outer sides of these motifs are bordered by a continuous key-fret band.[1]   With the exception of the rims where the light grey body is exposed, the bowl is covered with a neutral glaze with only the faintest tinge of blue in it.

(1) For comparable items, see Robert L. Hobson, *The Eumorfopoulos Collection*, Vol. II, London 1927, Pl. XI, B 36; and Jan Fontein, *The Charles B. Hoyt Collection*, Boston 1972, Pl. 72.

109 *JAR AND COVER*
Sung
10th to 13th century A.D.
Stoneware, Chün-yao
H. 2 in.　　　　*C-1034*

Both the cover and globular body of this miniature jar are covered with a thick bluish-green glaze.　The glaze stops short of the foot rim which was burned to a dark brown during firing.

110 *"BUD" VASE*
Sung
10th to 13th century A.D.
Stoneware, Chün-yao
H. 1 1/2 in.　　　*C-1011*

Shaped like a lobed fruit or the bud of a flower, this small container has a tiny aperture and stands on a short circular foot.　The light greenish-blue glaze, which turns into pale lavender where the lobes meet, stops short of the foot where the buff body is exposed.

111 *BOX AND COVER*
Sung
10th to 13th century A.D.
Stoneware, Chün-yao
Diam. 6 in.　　　*C-1041*

The upper and lower sections of this cylindrical box are almost identical in shape.[1] Two knobs located on either side of the mouth rim serve as guiding marks for proper closing of the box.　The small conical hole located in the center of the cover may have been used for the insertion of a tassel.　Except for the foot and mouth rims, the entire box is covered with a soft, thick and unctuous glaze of bluish-grey color.[2]

(1)　Published: *Catalogue of the International Exhibition of Chinese Art 1935–6*, London, fig. 1094.
(2)　See also S. Yorke Hardy, *Tung, Ju, Kuan, Chün, Kuang-tung and Glazed I-hsing Wares in the Percival David Foundation of Chinese Art*, London 1953, fig. 42 for a similar box.

112 *BOWL*

Sung
10th to 13th century A.D.
Stoneware, Chün-yao
H. 6 $^1/_2$ in.   Diam. 7 $^1/_4$ in.   C-1088

This large bowl with rounded sides stands on a small, but sturdy foot.   The thick, opalescent and heavily crackled bluish-green glaze covers the entire bowl, but stops short of the foot.

113 *PLATE*

Sung
10th to 13th century A.D.
Stoneware, "Green" Chün-yao
Diam. 7 ¹/₄ in.   *C-1014*

Except for the foot rim where the grey body is exposed, this plate is covered with a greenish-grey glaze which is highly vitrified and contains an unusual network of crackles forming parallel lines.[1]

(1)   For a similar plate, see Jean-Pierre Dubosc, *Exhibition of Chinese Art*, Venice 1954, fig. 470.

114 *BOWL*

Yüan
Ca. 14th century A.D.
Stoneware, Chün-yao
Diam. 4 ⁵/₈ in.   *C-1043*

This small "bubble" bowl stands on a fairly high circular foot which is robust and meticulously carved.   A thick, opalescent, lavender-blue glaze covers both the inside and outside of the bowl.   Darkening towards the mouth rim, it stops short of the foot which was burned to a reddish-brown during firing.   There are two purple splashes on the inside.[1]

(1)   Compare for instance, *The Arts of the Sung Dynasty [an Exhibition Held in the Arts Council Galleries June 16-July 23, 1960]*, in *TOCS*, Vol. 32, London 1960, Pl. 23, fig. 59; and Michael Sullivan, *Chinese Ceramics, Bronzes and Jades in the Collection of Sir Alan and Lady Barlow*, London 1963, fig. 40-b.

115 *DISH*

Northern Sung
10th to 11th century A.D.
Porcelaneous Northern Brown Ware
Diam. 6 3/4 in.   *C-1047*

This small dish has an everted six-foil rim and stands on a small, circular, finely carved foot with sharp edges.   The thick, finely crazed brown glaze stops short of the foot which reveals a buff body.[1]

(1) Compare *The Arts of the Sung Dynasty* [*an Exhibition Held in the Arts Council Galleries June 16-July 23, 1960*] in *TOCS*, Vol. 32, London 1960, Pl. 34, fig. 79.

116   *TEA BOWL*

Sung
10th to 13th century A.D.
Stoneware, Chien-yao
Diam. 4 3/4 in.   *C-1038*

This conical bowl is slightly constricted below the rim, which is bound in a ring of silver.   The foot is small, shallow and neatly carved.   A thick lustrous glaze of intense purplish-black color with silvery streaks covers both sides of the bowl and stops short of the foot in an irregular thick welt.   Where exposed, the body is hard blackish-brown.[1]

(1)   For a similar piece, see Robert L. Hobson, *The Eumorfopoulos Collection*, Vol. II, London 1927, Pl. LXXI, B 20 and 21.

117 *BOWL*
Sung
10th to 13th century A.D.
Stoneware, Tz'u-chou type, probably from Honan
Diam. 6 ³/₈ in.   *C-1007*

With the exception of the foot rim and base, the entire surface of this conical bowl with rounded sides is covered with a black, lustrous glaze.   The interior is decorated with five large iron-brown splashes. [1]   The body as revealed at the base is buff.

(1)   Compare with Roger Goepper et al., *Form und Farbe*, Tokyo 1972, fig. 116.

118 *BOWL*

Sung
10th to 13th century A.D.
Stoneware, Tz'u-chou type, probably from Honan
Diam. 6 ³/₈ in.   *C-1006*

The mouth of this conical bowl with rounded sides is slightly constricted below the rim.   The black glaze stops short of the base in an uneven line.   It is mottled with brown and blue spots on the lip, and·in the interior of the bowl there are five iron spots that were probably applied with a thick brush.   Where revealed, the body is buff.[1]

(1)   For a comparable item, see Robert L. Hobson, *The Eumorfopoulos Collection*, Vol. II, London 1927, Pl. LXVI, B 265.

119   *BOWL*

Sung
10th to 13th century A.D.
Stoneware, Tz'u-chou type
Diam. 5 ¹/₂ in.   C-1035

Of conical shape, this bowl rests on a small and sturdy foot.   The buff stoneware is covered by a thick, lustrous black glaze, except for the foot, which is unglazed, and the rim, where a neutral glaze has been applied over a ³/₈ inch wide band coated with a white slip.[1]

(1)   For a similar piece, see Hasebe Gakuji, *Tōji Zenshū*, No. 13, *Sō no Ji-shū Yō*, Tokyo 1958, Pl. 56; see also John Ayers, *The Seligman Collection of Oriental Art*, Vol. II, London 1964, D 134; and John Ayers, *The Baur Collection, Chinese Ceramics*, Vol. 1, Geneva 1968, A53, No. 229 and A62, No. 135 for a discussion of this type of ware.

120   *SMALL JAR*

Sung
10th to 13th century A.D.
Stoneware, Tz'u-chou type, probably from Honan
H. 3 ³/₄ in.   C-1015

The globular body opens on a wide mouth.   The base is recessed.   Except for the foot rim and part of the base, the reddish-brown stoneware is covered by a rich black glaze.   The three russet-colored splashes on the neck and shoulder were painted on the glaze in ferruginous brown slip.[1]

(1)   For another jar of similar shape and technique, see Henry Trubner, *Chinese Ceramics from the Prehistoric Period through Ch'ien Lung*, Los Angeles 1952, fig. 205.

121 *BOTTLE-SHAPED JAR*

Sung
10th to 13th century A.D.
Stoneware, Tz'u-chou type, probably from Honan
H. 7 in.   *C-1010*

The ovoid body of this small jar rests on a flat base and curves up to a small constricted neck with a large everted lip.   With the exception of the base and a small irregular band at the foot, the grey stoneware is covered with a black, lustrous glaze.   Five groups of four iron-brown spots are located on the shoulder at more or less regular intervals.

122 *BOTTLE-SHAPED JAR*

Sung
10th to 13th century A.D.
Stoneware, Tz'u-chou type, probably from Honan
H. 7 in.   *C-1009*

This small jar has a globular body and a small neck that looks like a miniature bowl. The recessed base is further depressed in its center. The buff stoneware is exposed at the foot rim. The rest of the vessel, including the base, is covered with a lustrous black-brown glaze. The three conventionalized bird motifs that decorate the bulging sides are painted in iron-brown slip.[1]

(1) For pieces that are similar in shape and technique, see for instance: Henry Trubner, *Chinese Ceramics from the Prehistoric Period through Ch'ien Lung*, Los Angeles 1952, fig. 206; James Cahill, *The Art of Southern Sung China*, New York 1962, fig. 98; and Michael Sullivan, *Chinese Ceramics, Bronzes and Jades in the Collection of Sir Alan and Lady Barlow*, London 1963, Pl. 49-b.

123 *JAR*

Sung
10th to 13th century A.D.
Stoneware, Tz'u-chou type, probably from Honan
H. 10 ¹/₂ in.   *C-1045*

The high, slightly recessed neck of this jar is equipped with four equidistant "pinched" handles. The high-shouldered ovoid body rests on a shallow ring foot with a slightly recessed base. The dome-shaped and somewhat warped lid is topped by a small hemispherical knob. The coarse grey stoneware is covered with a thick, lustrous black glaze that stops well above the foot in a neat, clear-cut line. With the exception of a narrow band around the neck, the inside of the jar is unglazed.

124 *VASE*

Sung
11th to 12th century A.D.
Tz'u-chou type glazed pottery
H. 7 ³/₈ in.   *C-105*

Of baluster shape, this vase has a foliated mouth and a tall, conical hollow foot. The shoulder and belly are respectively decorated with three small and three large floral medallions covered with a green glaze. The rest of the central zone is glazed in brown, while the neck, mouth and foot are mostly green. Both green and brown glazes were applied over a white slip and are faintly iridescent.[1] The clay itself is red.

(1)   A vase of similar shape and attributed to the Northern Sung period was published by Koyama Fujio in *Chūgoku Tōji, Jō*, Vol. 2 in the series *Idemitsu Bijutsukan Sensho*, Tokyo 1970, Pl. 35; see also Jan Fontein, *The Charles B. Hoyt Collection*, Boston 1972, Pl. 95.

125 *BOWL*

Sung
10th to 13th century A.D.
Glazed stoneware
Diam. 5 1/4   C-1036

This thickly potted conical bowl rests on a large, sturdy foot. It is covered on the inside with a finely crazed yellowing glaze. On the outside the same glaze covers only the upper part so that the unglazed lower part reveals a buff body. The inside displays a design of stylized flowers and ferns (?) that were painted in underglaze green.[1]   Parts of the design were burnt during the firing process.

(1) Published: H. F. E. Visser, *Asiatic Art in Private Collections of Holland and Belgium*, Amsterdam 1948, Pl. 133, No. 242.

126 *BOWL*

Southern Sung
12th to 13th century A.D.
Porcelain, Kuan ware
Diam. 3 7/8 in.   C-1050

This deep "lotus bowl" has fluted and foliate sides. It stands on a relatively high and splaying foot. The dark grey clay is exposed at the foot rim which is unglazed. The rest of the bowl is covered with an ash-grey crackled glaze.[1]

(1) Published: Harry M. Garner, "Ju and Kuan Wares," *Burlington Magazine*, Vol. 94, December 1952, Pl. 62. For another piece in the same series, see also Jean-Pierre Dubosc, *Exhibition of Chinese Art*, Venice 1954, fig. 452.

127 *FEEDING BOWL FOR A BIRD CAGE*

Sung
10th to 13th century A.D.
Porcelain, Kuan ware
H. 1 5/8 in.   C-1052

Of conical shape, this bowl has a pointed base, a small circular mouth and a ring-handle at one side. The entire piece is covered with a loosely crazed opaque glaze of green-blue color with the exception of the mouth rim which reveals a reddish-brown body.[1]

(1) For a similar shape, see Michael Sullivan, *Chinese Ceramics, Bronzes and Jades in the Collection of Sir Alan and Lady Barlow*, London 1963, Pl. 86-b.

128 *BOWL*

Koryo
12th century A.D.
Porcelaneous ware, Celadon
Diam. 6 $^3/_4$ in.   *K-8*

This conical bowl has rounded sides curving inwards slightly towards the rim and rests on a shallow circular foot.   The outside is ribbed and decorated with a carved design of overlapping petals.   The entire bowl is covered with a grey-green glaze.   Three spur marks are visible on the recessed base.[1]

(1) Compare with Robert P. Griffing, Jr., *The Art of the Korean Potter*, The Asia Society, Inc., New York 1968, fig. 40.

129 *WINE POT*

Koryo
12th century A.D.
Porcelaneous ware, Inlaid Celadon
H. 6 in.   *K-7*

The spherical body rests on a shallow foot. The S-shaped spout and spiraling three-stranded handle were modeled separately and applied to the body. The base of the slender, truncated neck is surrounded by a band of square meanders in low relief. Immediately below the mouth rim and on the shoulder are two narrow bands incised with square meanders and floral scrolls respectively. The base of the spout is incised with a floral pattern. The rest of the decoration consists of four peony sprays on the shoulder and four large semicircular frames containing other peony sprays.[1] All these motifs are made of black and white inlaid clays, as are the white double lines that frame the incised floral scrolls on the shoulder and the black key-fret border around the foot. The entire piece is covered with a lightly crazed greyish-green celadon glaze, but some small exposed spots on the base reveal a reddish-brown clay.

(1) For similar peony sprays, see Robert P. Griffing, Jr., *The Art of the Korean Potter*, The Asia Society, Inc., New York 1968, figs. 54 and 55.

130 *OIL BOTTLE*
Koryo
12th century A.D.
Porcelaneous ware, Inlaid Celadon
H. 2 1/4 in.   *K-1*

The globular body rests on a concave base.   The neck, short and narrow, is surmounted by a cup-shaped mouth.   The inlaid decoration consists of three black and white peony sprays evenly spaced on the shoulder.   The bottle is covered with a greyish-green celadon glaze with the exception of the base which reveals a grey body that has partially turned reddish-brown during firing. [1]

(1)   Compare with Gregory Henderson, *Korean Ceramics,* [*an Exhibition Held February 9– March 9, 1969, Divisions of Art Gallery*, The Ohio State University], Columbus [1969], fig. 66.

131 *BOWL*
Koryo
12th to 13th century A.D.
Porcelaneous ware, Inlaid Celadon
Diam. 4 3/4 in.   *K-9*

This deep bowl with rounded sides rests on a small circular foot and is elaborately decorated inside and outside with geometric, floral and animal motifs made of white and black inlaid clays.   The decoration of the interior consists of a band of floral scrolls, a wider band showing four cranes flying against a background of cloud scrolls and in the center a large chrysanthemum motif.   The exterior of the bowl is decorated with a border of minute, highly stylized clouds with four cranes in flight.   Below this border the main zone of decoration consists of four medallions containing black and white chrysanthemums evenly spaced within a field of leaf scrolls.   A third band, located just above the foot is made of black and white overlapping lotus petals.   The entire bowl is covered with a greyish-green celadon glaze, and there are three spur marks on the foot rim. [1]

(1)   For bowls with a somewhat similar exterior decoration, see Robert P. Griffing, Jr., *The Art of the Korean Potter*, The Asia Society, Inc., New York 1968, figs. 61 and 62.

Chronology

China

Ca. 2500–1500 B.C.	NEOLITHIC PERIOD	
Ca. 1523–1028	SHANG (YIN)	
Ca. 1027– 222	CHOU	
	Western Chou	Ca. 1027–771
	Eastern Chou	
	Ch'un-ch'iu	770–481
	Warring States	480–222
221– 207	CH'IN	
206 B.C.– 220 A.D.	HAN	
	Western Han	206 B.C.– 8 A.D.
	Hsin	9– 24 A.D.
	Eastern Han	25–220
221– 589	THE THREE KINGDOMS AND SIX DYNASTIES	
581– 618	SUI	
618– 906	T'ANG	
907– 960	FIVE DYNASTIES	
907–1124	LIAO	
960–1279	SUNG	
	Northern Sung	960–1127
	Southern Sung	1127–1279
1279–1368	YÜAN	
1368–1644	MING	
1644–1911	CH'ING	

Korea

Ca. 3rd Millennium B.C.–3rd Century B.C.	PREHISTORY
108 B.C.– 313 A.D.	LO-LANG
57 B.C.– 668 A.D.	THE THREE KINGDOMS
668– 935	UNITED SILLA
918–1392	KORYO
1392–1910	YI

Abbreviations Used in Text

ACASA   *Archives of the Chinese Art Society of America*, New York
BMFEA   *Bulletin of the Museum of Far Eastern Antiquities*, Stockholm
TOCS   *Transactions of the Oriental Ceramic Society*, London

Selected Bibliography

Addis, John, "Chinese Porcelain Found in the Philippines," *TOCS*, Vol. 37, 1967–69, London 1970, pp. 17–36.

Ayers, John, *The Seligman Collection of Oriental Art*, Vol. II, London 1964.
The Baur Collection Chinese Ceramics, Vol. 1, Geneva [1968].

Bunkazaihogoiinkai, *Kokuhō Jiten*, Tokyo 1961.
文化財保護委員會 國寶辭典. 東京 1961

Cahill, James, *The Art of Southern Sung China*, [*Exhibition at Asia House, 1962*], The Asia Society, New York 1962.

Catalogue of the Archaeological Collection in the Museum of the Faculty of Letters, Kyoto University, Part 3, Kyoto 1963.

Catalogue of the International Exhibition of Chinese Art, Royal Academy of Arts, November 1935–March 1936, London 1936.

Ch'en, Wan-li, *Chung-kuo Ch'ing Tz'u Shih-lüeh*, Hong Kong 1972.
陳萬里 中國青磁史略 香港 1972

Cheng, Te-k'un, *Archaeological Studies in Szechwan*, Cambridge 1957.

Chiang, Hsüan-tai, and Ch'in, T'ing-yü, *Chung-kuo Tz'u-ch'i te Fa-ming*, Shanghai 1956.
蔣玄佁 秦廷棫 中國瓷器的發明 上海 1956

Ch'in, T'ing-yü, *Chung-kuo Ku-tai T'ao-su I-shu*, Shanghai 1955.
秦廷棫 中國古代陶塑藝術 上海 1955

Ch'üan-kuo Chi-pen Chien-she Kung-ch'eng Chung Ch'u-t'u Wen-wu Chan-lan T'u-lu, Shanghai 1955.
全國基本建設工程中出土文物展覽圖錄 上海 1955

d'Argencé, René-Yvon Lefebvre, "The Magic World of the Chinese Bronze [in the Avery Brundage Collection]," *Apollo*, Vol. LXXXIV, No. 54, August 1966, pp. 113–125.
Chinese Ceramics in the Avery Brundage Collection, [San Francisco 1967].
Chinese Treasures from the Avery Brundage Collection, The Asia Society, Inc., New York 1968.

Dubosc, Jean-Pierre, *Exhibition of Chinese Art*, Venice 1954.

Fontein, Jan, *The Charles B. Hoyt Collection*, Boston 1972.

Garner, Harry M., "Ju and Kuan Wares," *Burlington Magazine*, Vol. 94, December 1952, pp. 348–353.

Goepper, Roger, et al., *Form und Farbe; Chinesische Bronzen und Früh-Keramik*, Cologne 1972.

van Goidsenhoven, Jacques P., *La Céramique Chinoise*, Brussels 1954.

Gompertz, G. St. G. M., *Chinese Celadon Wares*, London 1958.

Griffing, Robert P., Jr., *The Art of the Korean Potter*, The Asia Society, Inc., New York 1968.

Gyllensvärd, Bo, *Chinese Gold and Silver in the Carl Kempe Collection*, [Stockholm 1953].
Chinese Ceramics in the Carl Kempe Collection, Stockholm 1964.
Chinese Gold, Silver and Porcelain, The Kempe Collection, [New York 1971].

Gyllensvärd, Bo, and Pope, John Alexander, *Chinese Art from the Collection of H. M. King Gustaf VI Adolf of Sweden*, New York 1966.

Tokyo Imperial Household Museum, *Relics of Han and Pre-Han Dynasties; Catalogue of the Exhibition Held in May 1932 [in] the Imperial Household Museum*, Tokyo 1932.
帝室博物館　周漢遺寶　東京 1932

Hardy, S. Yorke, *Tung, Ju, Kuan, Chün, Kuang-tung and Glazed I-hsing Wares in the Percival David Foundation of Chinese Art*, London 1953.

Hasebe, Gakuji, *Tōji Zenshū*, No. 13, *Sō no Ji-shū Yō*, Tokyo 1958.
長谷部樂爾陶器全集 13　宋の磁州窯　東京 1958

Hayashiya, Seizō, and Hasebe, Gakuji, *Chinese Ceramics*, Tokyo 1966.
長谷部樂爾　林屋晴三　中國古陶磁　東京 1971

Henderson, Gregory, *Korean Ceramics*, [*An Exhibition Held February 9–March 9, 1969, Divisions of Art Gallery, The Ohio State University*], Columbus [1969].

Hobson, Robert L., *The Eumorfopoulos Collection*, Vols. I–II, London 1926.

Jettmar, Karl, *Art of the Steppes*, New York 1967.

Karlgren, Bernhard, "Huai and Han," *BMFEA*, No. 13, Stockholm 1941, entire issue. *A Catalogue of the Chinese Bronzes in the Alfred F. Pillsbury Collection*, Minneapolis 1953. "Chinese Agraffes in Two Swedish Collections," *BMFEA*, No. 38, Stockholm 1966, pp. 83–192.

Ko Chin, "Ching-yang Kao-chia-pao Tsao Chou Mu Tsang Fa-chüeh Chi," *Wen Wu*, No. 7, 1972.
葛今「涇陽高家堡早周墓葬掘記」文物 1972 年第 7 期.

Kobayashi, Taichirō, *Tōki Zenshū*, No. 12 *Tō Sō no Hakuji*, Tokyo 1957.
小林太市郎　陶器全集　12 唐宋の白磁　東京 1957

Koyama, Fujio, *Idemitsu Bijutsukan Sensho*, Vol. 2, *Chūgoku Tōji, Jō*, Tokyo 1970.
小山冨士夫　出光美術館選書　中國陶磁上　東京 1970

Kuroda, Genji and Sugimura, Yūzō, *Tōki Zenshū*, No. 14, *Ryō no Tōji*, Tokyo 1958.
黒田源次　杉村勇造　陶器全集 14　遼の陶磁　東京 1958

Lindberg, Gustaf, "Hsing-yao and Ting-yao," *BMFEA*, No. 25, Stockholm 1953, pp. 19–71.

Liu, T'i-chih, compiler, *Hsiao Chiao Ching Ko Chih Shih Wen Tzu*, Vol. 4 [n.p., Pref. 1935].
留體智輯　小校經閣金石文字己亥年

Lo, Chen-yü, *Chen Sung T'ang Chi Ku I Wen*, Vol. 4, Chang-chou 1931.
羅振玉　貞松堂集古遺文

Locsin, Leandro and Cecilia, *Oriental Ceramics Discovered in the Philippines*, Rutland [1967].

Loehr, Max, *Relics of Ancient China from the Collection of Dr. Paul Singer*, The Asia Society, Inc., [New York 1965].

Lovell, Hin-cheung, *Illustrated Catalogue of Ting Yao and Related White Wares in the Percival David Foundation of Chinese Art*, [London] 1964.

Mahler, Jane Gaston, *The Westerners among the Figurines of the T'ang Dynasty of China*, Rome 1959.

Matsubara, Saburō, *Chinese Buddhist Sculpture*, Tokyo 1966.
松原三郎　中國佛教彫刻史研究　東京 1966

Mizuno, Seiichi, *Tōki Zenshū*, No. 25, *Tō San-sai*, Tokyo 1965.
水野清一　陶器全集 25　唐三彩　東京 1965

Osaka Museum and The Center of Asian Art and Culture, *Osaka Exchange Exhibition, Paintings from the Abe Collection and Other Masterpieces of Chineses Art*, Osaka and San Francisco 1970.

Paine, Robert Treat, Jr., *The Charles B. Hoyt Collection Memorial Exhibition, February 13–March 30, 1952*, Boston [1952].

Palmgren, Nils, *Selected Chinese Antiquities from the Collection of Gustaf Adolf, Crown Prince of Sweden*, Stockholm 1948.

Pope, John Alexander, et al., *The Freer Chinese Bronzes*, Vol. 1, Washington 1967.

Prodan, Mario, *The Art of the T'ang Potter*, New York [1961, c. 1960].

Rostovtsev, Mikhail I., *The Animal Style in South Russia and China*, Princeton 1929.

Rowland, Benjamin, Jr., *The Evolution of the Buddha Image*, [*Catalogue of an Exhibition, 8 May–30 June 1963*], The Asia Society, Inc., [New York 1963].

The Royal Tomb of Wang Chien of the Former Shu, Peking 1964.

Salmony, Alfred, *Sammlung J. E. H. Menten, Chinesische Grabfunde und Bronzen*, Zurich 1948.
Sino-Siberian Art in the Collection of C. T. Loo, Paris 1933.

Satō, Masahiko, *Chūgoku no Dogū*, Tokyo 1965.
佐藤雅彦 中國の土偶 東京1965

Schloss, Ezekiel, *Foreigners in Ancient Chinese Art*, New York 1969.

Sekai Bijutsu Zenshū, Vol. 13, *Chūgoku*, Part 2, Tokyo 1962.
世界美術全集 中國 東京1962

Sekai Kōkogaku Taikei, Vol. 7, *Higashi Ajia*, Part III, Tokyo 1963.
世界考古學大系 東アジア 東京1963

Sekai Tōji Zenshū, Vol. 8, *From Ancient China to Six Dynasties*, Tokyo 1955.
世界陶磁全集 東京1955

Sekai Tōji Zenshū, Vol. 9, *Sui and T'ang Dynasties*, Tokyo 1956.
世界陶磁全集 東京1956

Sekai Tōji Zenshū, Vol. 10, *Sung and Liao Dynasties*, Tokyo 1955.
世界陶磁全集 東京1955

Singer, Paul, "Some Puzzle Pieces," *Oriental Art*, Vol. XVIII, No. 2, Summer 1972, pp. 155–162.

Soper, Alexander, "Chinese Sculpture [in the Avery Brundage Collection,"] *Apollo*, Vol. LXXXIV, No. 54, August 1966, pp. 103–112.

Sullivan, Michael, *Chinese Ceramics, Bronzes and Jades in the Collection of Sir Alan and Lady Barlow*, London 1963.

Tokyo National Museum, *Illustrated Catalogue of Old Oriental Ceramics Donated by Mr. Yokogawa*, Tokyo 1953.

Trubner, Henry, *The Arts of the T'ang Dynasty*, Los Angeles 1957.
Chinese Ceramics from the Prehistoric Period through Ch'ien Lung, Los Angeles, 1952.

TOCS, Vol. 32, *The Arts of the Sung Dynasty*, [*an Exhibition Held in the Arts Council Galleries, June 16–July 23, 1960*], London 1960.

Tseng, Hsien-chi, and Dart, Robert Paul, *The Charles B. Hoyt Collection*, Vol. 1, Boston 1964.

Umehara, Sueji, *Selected Ancient Mirrors Found at Shao-hsing Tombs*, Kyoto 1939.
Selected Relics of Ancient Chinese Bronzes from Collections in Japan, Vol. II, Osaka 1940.
Shina Kodō Seika, Vol. II, Osaka 1960.
支那古銅精華 梅原末治 大阪1933–5

Visser, H. F. E., *Asiatic Art in Private Collections of Holland and Belgium*, Amsterdam 1948.

Wang Shih-lun, *Che-chiang Ch'u-t'u T'ung Ching Hsüan-chi*, Peking 1957.
王士論 浙江出土銅鏡選集 北京

Warner, Langdon, *Pacific Cultures*, San Francisco 1939.

Watson, William, *Ancient Chinese Bronzes*, London 1962.

Wen-wu Ch'u-pan-she, *Wen-hua Ta Ke-ming Ch'i-chien Ch'u-t'u Wen-wu*, Vol. 1, Peking 1972.
文物出版社 文化大革命期間出土文物

Wirgin, Jan, "Sung Ceramic Designs," *BMFEA* No. 42, Stockholm 1970, pp. 1–272.

Yetts, W. Perceval, *The Cull Chinese Bronzes*, London 1939.